Plone 3.3 Site Administration

Manage your site like a Plone professional

Alex Clark

BIRMINGHAM - MUMBAI

Plone 3.3 Site Administration

First published: July 2010

Production Reference: 1170710

Published by Packt Publishing Ltd.
32 Lincoln Road
Olton
Birmingham, B27 6PA, UK.

ISBN 978-1-847197-04-7

www.packtpub.com

Cover Image by Ed Maclean (edmaclean@gmail.com)

Credits

Author
Alex Clark

Reviewer
Steve McMahon

Acquisition Editor
Rashmi Phadnis

Development Editor
Darshana Shinde

Technical Editor
Krutika V. Katelia

Indexer
Monica Ajmera Mehta

Editorial Team Leader
Mithun Sehgal

Project Team Leader
Priya Mukherji

Project Coordinator
Zainab Bagasrawala

Proofreader
Lynda Sliwoski

Graphics
Geetanjali Sawant

Production Coordinator
Melwyn D'sa

Cover Work
Melwyn D'sa

Foreword

Back in the old days, Zope was a big monolithic Python package that contained the entire web framework. Creating and customizing a **Plone site** was accomplished by adding "Products" (special Python packages that only Zope 2 understands) to a special directory. When Zope 2 launched, it would scan this directory and look for special initialization functions to activate each Product. This plugin-based approach was nice in some ways, but not nice in others.

For example, how can you efficiently manage your web applications when installing means you need to manually unzip hundreds of Products on to your filesystem, and make sure all the Product dependencies were satisfied? This was a nightmare!

I remember some Zope sprints back in 2002 where we had to set up specific Zope environments to work. We had to go through every Product's README to list all its dependencies, and make sure we had all of them, whether they were other Products or Python packages. That usually took us half a day before we could start coding.

Nowadays, setting up any kind of Plone-based application can be performed automatically in a few minutes, thanks to **zc.buildout**! This tool reads a configuration file, sets up your environment by downloading Python packages from the Python Package Index, and performs any additional steps as needed.

But zc.buildout, and all its underlying technology, like Distribute or Distutils, takes a long time to understand and master. It's not the silver bullet either — there are traps all along the road. Plus, it may compete with your server's own packaging system, which sometimes can be an issue.

But the pain is worthwhile! Learning all these tools that became a standard in the Plone community will give you all the power you need to set up and manage industrial-level Plone sites.

And what's great is that the Zope and Plone communities have now adopted the Python Distutils standard as a basis for their building blocks, making it easier to share code between the two worlds.

That is what this book is all about!

Alex, who is a brilliant Plone site administrator and developer, will guide you through the whole process, from setting up your Python environment, to installing, upgrading, and managing your Plone applications with ease, and avoiding pitfalls along the way.

Enjoy! (And keep it under your pillow.)

Tarek Ziadé, Turcey, France, May 2010
Python core developer and Distribute maintainer
http://ziade.org

About the Author

Alex Clark is a Plone consultant from Bethesda, MD, USA. He currently operates a busy open source consulting firm, along with his wife and business partner, Amy Clark. He also operates a non-profit organization that supports the local Python developer community by organizing monthly meetings, trainings, sprints, conferences, and more. For more information, please see http://aclark.net and http://zpugdc.org respectively.

Alex is a co-author of *"Practical Plone 3"*, *Packt Publishing* (https://www.packtpub.com/practical-plone-3-beginners-guide-to-building-powerful-websites/book) and this book marks his first sole authorship. He hopes it will empower individuals, organizations and the world to use and contribute to Plone!

I would like to thank the following people for their assistance in writing this book: Amy Clark, Chris McDonough, Chris Shenton, Darshana Shinde, David Glick, Erik Rose, Fernando Correa Neto, Gilles Lenfant, Hanno Schichting, Krutika Katelia, Martin Aspeli, Matt Bowen, Matthew Wilkes, Michael Dunlap, Rashmi Phadnis, Reed O'Brien, Ricardo Newbery, Steve McMahon, Tarek Ziadé, Veda Williams, Wichert Akkerman, Zainab Bagasrawala, and you, if I forgot to thank you!

Also, I would be remiss if I did not thank the giants whose shoulders I am fortunate enough to stand on every day: Guido Van Rossum for Python, Jim Fulton for Zope, and Alexander Limi and Alan Runyan for Plone. Thank you!

About the Reviewer

Steve McMahon is a partner in Reid-McMahon, LLC, a Davis, California, web development company specializing in deploying Plone for non-profit and governmental organizations. He is chief maintainer for Plone's "Unified" and OS X installers and release manager for the popular PloneFormGen add-on. Steve is serving his third term on the Plone Foundation Board of Directors and his second as board secretary. He also does extensive volunteer work for the Davis Community Network, where he helps build local community with Internet resources.

Steve was one of the many authors of *"Practical Plone 3"*, *Packt Publishing* (`https://www.packtpub.com/practical-plone-3-beginners-guide-to-building-powerful-websites/book`) and has been a technical reviewer for several Plone books.

For my other half, Amy Elyse.

Table of Contents

Preface

Plone is a powerful web application used mainly for website content management and comprised of many different, but related Python packages. But it wasn't always this way.

Over the years, Plone has grown from just a few packages built on top of the powerful Zope 2 application server, while Zope 2 itself has grown from a single, monolithic package to a collection of smaller, and often reusable Python packages.

All of this hardly matters to Plone's end users, but unfortunately it has been difficult to hide such details from them. Some day that goal may be achieved, but in the meantime there is this book, which aims to clear up some of the confusion.

That confusion mostly surrounds the use of a tool called Buildout, which is used to assemble the various Python packages. Buildout is a fantastic tool for developers, but not such a good choice for end users.

That said, if you are interested in learning about Buildout and how to use it to build Plone sites, then this book is for you.

What this book covers

Chapter 1, *Background* introduces you to Python, the version that may already be on your computer, or the version you may choose to install if it is not. After Python installation, installation of various tools such as Distribute, PIP, and Buildout is covered. Finally, an installation of Python using Buildout is covered.

Chapter 2, *Site Basics* covers a variety of Plone site basics including the creation of the Plone site object itself (inside the Zope database), followed by some simple customizations of some of Plone's navigational elements and content types.

Chapter 3, *Appearance* covers the first thing everyone wants to do after installing Plone—change the appearance. In addition, various aspects of through the web versus filesystem theming are covered.

Chapter 4, *Administration* describes various mail settings used in development, plus users and groups management with out of the box features versus LDAP add-ons.

Chapter 5, *Deployment and Maintenance* starts off with the creation of a production buildout, in which various database and log-related tasks are incorporated and automated throughout.

Chapter 6, *Optimization* optimizes site deployments with various techniques to add caching agents, load balancers, process monitors, and performance analyzers.

Chapter 7, *Security* secures site deployments with various techniques to manage hosts, ports, users, permissions, and security fixes.

Chapter 8, *The Future* looks to the future with various techniques to ensure we can manage our buildouts successfully now, as well as one year from now.

What you need for this book

This book aims to take you through Plone site administration shortly after operating system installation. Some operating systems ship with Python, some don't. In either case, you will be escorted through Python installation and its basic use. This is followed by the rest of the story, which simply builds on top of Python. In other words, you will just need a modern computer and an operating system.

Who this book is for

This book is for folks who want to become more familiar with how to professionally manage their Plone sites, with techniques used by Python, Zope, and Plone professionals. That means everyone from content editors, to system administrators, to end users of Plone may be interested in the subject matter.

Ideally the reader will have some experience with Python and Plone already, but it is not strictly required.

Some basic computer skills are required, such as the ability to use a terminal window, text editor, and web browser.

Conventions

In this book, you will find a number of styles of text that distinguish between different kinds of information. Here are some examples of these styles, and an explanation of their meaning.

Code words in text are shown as follows: "If so, just create the directory and then re-run the `buildout` command."

A block of code is set as follows:

```
[buildout]
extends = buildout.cfg
parts += plonesite
[plonesite]
recipe = collective.recipe.plonesite
```

Next, we specify that we want the checkout to occur in the `src` directory (instead of the `parts` directory, which is the default) by setting the `location` parameter:

```
location = src
```

When we wish to draw your attention to a particular part of a code block, the relevant lines or items are set in bold:

```
[buildout]
extends = http://dist.plone.org/release/3.3.5/versions.cfg
versions = versions
parts =
    zope2
    instance
find-links =
    http://dist.plone.org/thirdparty/PILwoTk-1.1.6.4.tar.gz
```

Any command-line input or output is written as follows:

```
$ buildout -c 01-background-python.cfg
```

Some of the code lines were too long to fit on one line. In that case, you may see a back slash (\) like this to indicate that the next line is really a part of the current line of the code, for example:

```
urls=http://dist.plone.org/thirdparty/\
  PILwoTk-1.1.6.4.tar.gz
```

New terms and **important words** are shown in bold. Words that you see on the screen, in menus or dialog boxes for example, appear in the text like this: "Select the checkbox next to the **Plone site** object, and click on **Delete**."

Warnings or important notes appear in a box like this.

 Tips and tricks appear like this.

Reader feedback

Feedback from our readers is always welcome. Let us know what you think about this book—what you liked or may have disliked. Reader feedback is important for us to develop titles that you really get the most out of.

To send us general feedback, simply send an e-mail to feedback@packtpub.com, and mention the book title via the subject of your message.

If there is a book that you need and would like to see us publish, please send us a note in the **SUGGEST A TITLE** form on www.packtpub.com or e-mail suggest@packtpub.com.

If there is a topic that you have expertise in and you are interested in either writing or contributing to a book on, see our author guide on www.packtpub.com/authors.

Customer support

Now that you are the proud owner of a Packt book, we have a number of things to help you to get the most from your purchase.

 Downloading the example code for this book
You can download the example code files for all Packt books you have purchased from your account at http://www.PacktPub.com. If you purchased this book elsewhere, you can visit http://www.PacktPub.com/support and register to have the files e-mailed directly to you.

Errata

Although we have taken every care to ensure the accuracy of our content, mistakes do happen. If you find a mistake in one of our books—maybe a mistake in the text or the code—we would be grateful if you would report this to us. By doing so, you can save other readers from frustration and help us improve subsequent versions of this book. If you find any errata, please report them by visiting http://www.packtpub.com/support, selecting your book, clicking on the **let us know** link, and entering the details of your errata. Once your errata are verified, your submission will be accepted and the errata will be uploaded on our website, or added to any list of existing errata, under the Errata section of that title. Any existing errata can be viewed by selecting your title from http://www.packtpub.com/support.

Piracy

Piracy of copyrighted material on the Internet is an ongoing problem across all media. At Packt, we take the protection of our copyright and licenses very seriously. If you come across any illegal copies of our works, in any form, on the Internet, please provide us with the location address or website name immediately so that we can pursue a remedy.

Please contact us at copyright@packtpub.com with a link to the suspected pirated material.

We appreciate your help in protecting our authors, and our ability to bring you valuable content.

Questions

You can contact us at questions@packtpub.com if you are having a problem with any aspect of the book, and we will do our best to address it.

1
Background

In the past few years, the Plone community has experienced some dramatic changes in the way Plone sites are being developed, deployed, and maintained:

- Once upon a time, add-ons to Zope 2 were distributed as specialized Python packages (called **Products**); nowadays they are distributed as generic Python packages (called **Eggs**)

- Originally, the Zope 2 application server was distributed as a single monolithic package; nowadays many parts of Zope 2 have been factored out into smaller packages, which comprise a portion of a larger set of reusable Zope packages (called the **Zope Toolkit**)

To make things more challenging, the Zope community has recently renamed various projects and has redefined the Zope ecosystem in the process:

- The web framework formerly known as Zope 3 is now called **Bluebream** (http://bluebream.zope.org/)

- The set of libraries formerly known as Zope 3 is now called the **Zope Toolkit** (http://docs.zope.org/zopetoolkit/)

While this influx of new technology alongside the old has presented a challenge for many, it represents a fundamental step in the forward direction for Plone:

- With the adoption of Eggs, Plone joins the rest of the Python community in sharing a common packaging framework with a rich set of features, including the ability to specify version dependencies

- With the adoption of the Zope Toolkit, Plone joins the rest of the Zope community in using the Zope Component Architecture to manage application complexity

Unfortunately, there is a price to pay for all of this progress—confusion. Many people are confused about the best way to develop, deploy, and maintain their Plone site. This is very much expected with a complex system like Plone, but is not ideal.

 Although not quite there yet, Plone is moving rapidly towards a better development, deployment, and maintenance story. Every day the situation improves, and there has never been a better time to start using Plone! The author truly believes in the Plone software and community, and hopes this book will inspire others to feel the same.

By presenting clear instructions and using best practices and techniques from the Python and Zope communities, this book aims to eliminate any remaining confusion.

In this chapter, you will learn:

- Site administration essentials
- What you need to get started
- About the Plone installers
- About Python software distributions
- How to install **Distribute**—a framework for managing Python packages
- How to install **PIP**—a more user friendly Python package installer
- How to install **Buildout**—a tool for building software
- More about Python software distributions
- How to install a C compiler
- How to install **Subversion**—a version control system
- How to install Python with Buildout

Site administration essentials

Before we begin, let's put into perspective the effort we are about to undertake. Everything you learn in this book is intended to make you a better Plone site administrator.

In order to disseminate the subject matter, we will divide the site administrator's tasks into three categories:

- Development
- Deployment
- Maintenance

Development

Development usually begins with a buildout configuration file checked into a software repository. Initially, this buildout creates a software stack suitable for running the desired version of Plone.

Using this buildout, any developer can join the development team quickly and gain speed fairly easily. As the site administrator, you may be doing some, all, or none of the coding for your site, but you should still be familiar with the process.

Development tasks usually consist of:

- **Creation of a policy package**: It is necessary for performing various site customizations. Policy in this context usually means: "applies project-specific customizations or features". See Chapter 5 of *"Professional Plone Development"*, *Martin Aspeli, Packt Publishing* (https://www.packtpub.com/ Professional-Plone-web-applications-CMS/book) for more information.

- **Theme development**: Traditionally, themes are implemented within a theme package that contains CSS and JavaScript files, images, and so on. More recently, you may see Deliverance or XDV-based themes being used (outside of Plone). See *"Plone 3 Theming"*, *Veda Williams, Packt Publishing* (https://www.packtpub.com/plone-3-theming-create-flexible-powerful-professional-templates/book) for more information.

- **Adding features**: In addition to customizing Plone's default features, you may need to add new features as well. You can do this by installing existing add-ons or developing new features from scratch.

- **Writing tests**: Unless you want to click through your site every time you make a code change to make sure that everything still works properly, you will want to write the tests—you will want to write *lots* of tests. In addition to the practical aspects of testing, good test coverage is a strong indicator of a job well done. See: http://plone.org/documentation/kb/testing for more information.

Deployment

Eric S. Raymond (http://catb.org/~esr/), besides being a well-known open source advocate, is also well-known for this statement (http://www.catb. org/~esr/writings/cathedral-bazaar/cathedral-bazaar/ar01s04.html):

"Release early. Release often. And listen to your customers."

This sentiment is not lost on the professional Plone site administrator. The sooner you can deploy a basic set of features to staging, the happier your client or boss is going to be. Deployment steps usually consist of:

- Provision servers
- Deploy to staging
- Performance testing
- Client evaluation
- Deploy to production

Maintenance

These are the tasks that no one wants to perform, but that everyone will blame you for not doing whenever they are not done. Fortunately, we can automate most of these:

- Pack the database
- Rotate logs
- Back up the site
- Monitor performance

The following diagram illustrates the typical workflow associated with these tasks:

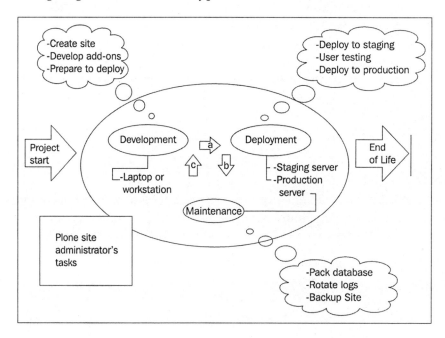

In the diagram above, you will notice three workflow states — development, deployment, and maintenance. We describe the common transitions between each of these states as follows:

a. **Development to deployment**: During development, a project buildout is created. Not long after that, it may be deployed to staging for testing. It is not uncommon to deploy to staging many times before deploying to production.

b. **Deployment to maintenance**: Eventually, after development is complete, deployment to production occurs. Once you deploy to production, proper maintenance becomes critical.

c. **Maintenance to development**: After some time in production (with regularly-scheduled maintenance), more development may be required to fix bugs or add new features. Eventually, the development costs may outweigh the return on investment, at which point you are approaching the end of life.

Do not take this too literally; it is just meant to provide some perspective and a glimpse into the cyclical nature of Plone site administration.

What you need to get started

Now let us bring the starting line into perspective, with a quote from Alice in Wonderland:

> *The White Rabbit put on his spectacles. "Where shall I begin, please your Majesty?" he asked. "Begin at the beginning", the King said gravely, "and go on till you come to the end: then stop."*

Our story begins at the beginning, with your computer, operating system, a terminal window, text editor, and hardly anything else.

Modern computer

You will need a modern computer, preferably one made in the last few years.

Supported operating system

While we cannot cover every operating system, we will try to cover three of the most popular ones:

- Mac OS X 10.6 (Snow Leopard)
- Windows 7
- Ubuntu Linux 10.04 (Lucid)

The previous operating systems are in no particular order!

While the author's desktop is Mac OS X, the techniques described in this book have been tested on Windows 7 and Ubuntu Linux 10.04 virtual machines running in parallel. We will assume you have only one OS, so feel free to skip the sections that are not applicable to you.

If you do not have one of these supported operating systems, a reasonable facsimile will probably do.

Internet connection

You will need a reasonably fast Internet connection, preferably cable, DSL, or any faster one to download the open source software discussed in this book.

Terminal window

We will make frequent use of the following:

- Terminal in Max OS X
- Command Prompt in Windows 7
- GNOME Terminal in Ubuntu Linux

Text editor

You should have a text editor, and be familiar with how to use it. If you need a suggestion, try one of these:

- **Mac OS X**: Textmate (`http://macromates.com/`, `$55 USD`)
- **Windows 7**: Notepad++ (`http://notepad-plus.sourceforge.net/uk/site.htm`, free)
- **Ubuntu Linux**: gedit (`http://projects.gnome.org/gedit/`, free, included with Ubuntu Linux)

If you are a programmer or a system administrator, you may be using Vi or Emacs already, and do not need the author's recommendation.

About Plone installers

In this book, we will be building Plone sites from the ground up, starting with Python.

However, we would be remiss if we did not mention the Plone installers. If you need a trouble-free demo, or if you just want to download something that works, look no further than `http://plone.org/products/plone`. You will find installers for each of our targeted operating systems:

 Windows installer (Windows 2000, 2003, XP, Vista, 7)
For Windows (32MB)

 OS X binary installer for Snow Leopard (64-bit)
For Mac OS X (26MB)

 OS X installer for Intel/PPC (10.4,10.5)
For Mac OS X

 Unified Installer - for Linux/BSD/OS X/UNIX/Solaris (compiles and installs Python, Zope and Plone plus dependencies for you)
For Linux/BSD/Unix (30MB)

Many people use these in production with great success (especially the **Unified Installer**).

However, if you want to know how the installers work, or if you need more flexibility than the installers can provide, you should keep reading.

And now, we shall begin.

About Python software distributions

With the exception of Windows, most modern operating systems ship with some version of Python pre-installed.

Although this version may not be compatible with Plone 3.3, it is still useful to have around.

In case Python is not pre-installed, you should install Python 2.4 because that version works with Plone 3.3. We will get to that later in the chapter.

Using Python on Mac OS X

Mac OS X 10.6 is shipped with Python 2.6 pre-installed. Although this version will not work with Plone 3.3, we can use it to install the following:

- Distribute
- PIP
- Buildout

But first, let us explore some basic Python usage.

Verify that Python works

To verify that Python works, open **Finder** | **Applications** | **Utilities** | **Terminal**.

1. **Check the version**: To check the version, type:

   ```
   $ python -V
   ```

2. **Run the interpreter**: To run the interactive Python interpreter, type:

   ```
   $ python
   ```

3. **Exit:** To exit, press *Ctrl + D*.

You should see:

```
$ python -V
Python 2.6.1
$ python
Python 2.6.1 (r261:67515, Feb 11 2010, 00:51:29)
[GCC 4.2.1 (Apple Inc. build 5646)] on darwin
Type "help", "copyright", "credits" or "license" for more information.
>>> ^D
$
```

We have just demonstrated using Python 2.6 on Mac OS X.

Installing Python on Windows

Windows 7 does not come pre-installed with Python, but there is an installer available on http://python.org.

Download the Python installer

Since an installer for the latest version (in the 2.4.x series) is not available, and because it is difficult to compile the source on Windows, we will use the 2.4.4 version instead.

Using Internet Explorer (or any other web browser):

1. Navigate to `http://www.python.org/download/releases/2.4.4/`.

2. Scroll down to Windows.

3. Select python-2.4.4.msi (`http://www.python.org/ftp/python/2.4.4/python-2.4.4.msi`).

4. Save the file.

Run the Python installer

Windows will present a series of dialogues which you can answer based on the following suggestions:

- Install for all users
- Install to the default location
- Install the default features

You should see:

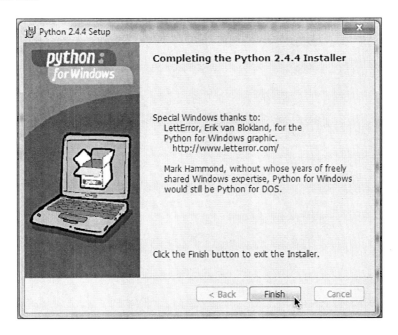

Configure the Environment Variable—Path

Now that Python is installed, we would like to be able to easily run the interactive Python interpreter from the Command Prompt. To accomplish this, perform the following steps:

1. Select **Start | Computer | System properties | Advanced system settings | Environment Variables**.

2. Under **System variables**, scroll down to **Path**.

3. Select **Edit**.

4. Add the following separated by a semicolon:
   - `C:\Python24`
   - `C:\Python24\Scripts`

5. Click on **Save**.

You should see:

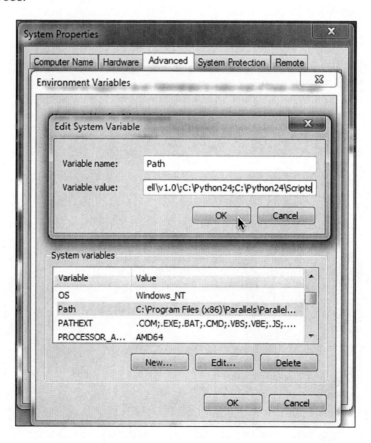

Now, let us test this.

Verify that Python works

To verify that Python works, open **Start | All Programs | Accessories | Command Prompt**.

1. **Check the version**: To check the version, type:

   ```
   $ python -V
   ```

2. **Run the interpreter**: To run the interactive Python interpreter, type:

   ```
   $ python
   ```

3. **Exit**: To exit, press *Ctrl* + *Z* and hit *Enter*.

You should see:

```
Administrator: Command Prompt
$ python -V
Python 2.4.4

$ python
Python 2.4.4 (#71, Oct 18 2006, 08:34:43) [MSC v.1310 32 bit (Intel)] on win32
Type "help", "copyright", "credits" or "license" for more information.
>>> ^Z

$ _
```

We have just finished demonstrating how to install and test Python 2.4 on Windows.

While we are here, let us take a minute to install some additional software that we will need later.

Install PyWin

If you were to install and run Plone now, you may encounter the following error:

```
C:\Users\Administrator\Developer\plone-site-admin\buildout>bin\instance.exe
Traceback (most recent call last):
  File "C:\Users\Administrator\Developer\plone-site-admin\buildout\bin\instance-
script.py", line 128, in ?
    import plone.recipe.zope2instance.ctl
  File "c:\users\administrator\developer\plone-site-admin\buildout\eggs\plone.re
cipe.zope2instance-3.6-py2.4.egg\plone\recipe\zope2instance\ctl.py", line 49, in
 ?
    import pywintypes
ImportError: No module named pywintypes
```

To avoid this error, install PyWin for Python 2.4:

1. Browse to `http://sourceforge.net/proje cts/pywin32/files/`.
2. Select `pywin32-214.win32-py2.4.exe` to download the file.
3. Run the installer.

The PyWin library provides access to the Windows programming API. Visit `http://plone.org/documentation/kb/using-buildout-on-windows/` for more information.

Using Python on Ubuntu Linux

Ubuntu Linux ships with Python 2.6 pre-installed.

All we need to do is test it.

Verify that Python works

To verify that Python works, open **Applications | Accessories | Terminal**.

1. **Check the version**: To check the version, type:

   ```
   $ python -V
   ```
2. **Run the interpreter**: To run the interactive Python interpreter, type:

   ```
   $ python
   ```
3. **Exit**: To exit, press *Ctrl + D*.

You should see:

We have just finished demonstrating how to test Python 2.4 on Ubuntu Linux.

At this point, we have taken steps to explore Python on each of our targeted operating systems.

We will now move forward with that technology.

How to install Distribute—a framework for managing Python packages

First, let us have a look at some background on Distribute. According to the Distribute website (`http://packages.python.org/distribute/`), Distribute is:

> *"... intended to replace Setuptools as the standard method for working with Python module distributions."*

According to the setuptools website (`http://peak.telecommunity.com/DevCenter/setuptools`), setuptools is:

> *"... a collection of enhancements to the Python distutils (for Python 2.3.5 and up on most platforms; 64-bit platforms require a minimum of Python 2.4) that allow you to more easily build and distribute Python packages, especially ones that have dependencies on other packages."*

Among other things, Distribute facilitates the easy installation of Python packages from the **Python Package Index (PyPI)** page on `http://pypi.python.org`.

The Distribute authors (also known as the **Fellowship of the Packaging**) enthusiastically recommend you choose Distribute over setuptools with this propaganda from their website (`http://packages.python.org/distribute/`):

In addition to fixing setuptools, the Fellowship of the Packaging plan to fix the core package management libraries in Python.

These two frameworks are built on top of the **Distutils** (http://docs.python.org/library/distutils.html) library, which is part of the Python core, and is distributed with Python.

In order to fix things properly, fixes must be applied at the Distutils level.

Fortunately, all the hard work done in Distutils, setuptools, and Distribute over the years will end up in a new library called Distutils 2.

If you are interested in the future of Python packaging, the following diagram (http://guide.python-distribute.org/introduction.html#current-state-of-packaging) may help explain the status quo:

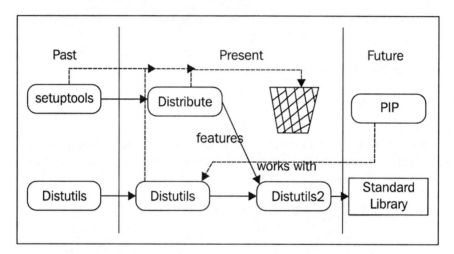

This diagram suggests we use the Distribute add-on library until Distutils 2 is released as part of the core library (which is months away, as of May 2010).

And now we shall install Distribute.

Installing Distribute on Mac OS X

While the **curl** program is recommended by the Distribute propaganda, it is not pre-installed with Mac OS X.

You can use Safari instead.

Download distribute_setup.py

To download the Distribute installer using Safari:

1. Browse to `http://python-distribute.org`.

2. Click on **distribute_setup.py**.

3. Select **File** | **Save as** and save it as `distribute_setup.py`.

Execute distribute_setup.py

To install Distribute, open **Finder** | **Applications** | **Utilities** | **Terminal**, change the directories to wherever you saved the file, and then type:

```
$ sudo python distribute_setup.py
```

If prompted, type your Mac OS X user account password.

You should see:

```
Installed /Library/Python/2.6/site-packages/distribute-0.6.12-py2.6.egg
Processing dependencies for distribute==0.6.12
Finished processing dependencies for distribute==0.6.12
After install bootstrap.
Creating /Library/Python/2.6/site-packages/setuptools-0.6c11-py2.6.egg-info
Creating /Library/Python/2.6/site-packages/setuptools.pth
$ 
```

Verify that Distribute works

To verify that Distribute works, open **Finder** | **Applications** | **Utilities** | **Terminal** and type:

```
$ easy_install
```

You should see:

```
$ easy_install
install_dir /Library/Python/2.6/site-packages/
error: No urls, filenames, or requirements specified (see --help)
$ 
```

This means Distribute is installed and working.

We have just finished demonstrating how to install and test Distribute on Mac OS X.

Installing Distribute on Windows 7

The curl program does not ship with Windows, but you can use Internet Explorer instead.

Download distribute_setup.py

To download the Distribute installer with Internet Explorer:

1. Browse to `http://python-distribute.org`.
2. Right-click on **distribute_setup.py**.
3. Select **Save Target As** and save it as `distribute_setup.py`.

Execute distribute_setup.py

To install Distribute, select **Start | All Programs | Accessories | Command Prompt** and type:

```
$ python distribute_setup.py
```

You should see:

```
Installed c:\python24\lib\site-packages\distribute-0.6.12-py2.4.egg
Processing dependencies for distribute==0.6.12
Finished processing dependencies for distribute==0.6.12
After install bootstrap.
Creating C:\Python24\Lib\site-packages\setuptools-0.6c11-py2.4.egg-info
Creating C:\Python24\Lib\site-packages\setuptools.pth
$
```

Verify that Distribute works

To verify that Distribute works, select **Start | All Programs | Accessories | Command Prompt** and type:

```
> easy_install
```

You should see:

```
$ easy_install
install_dir C:\Python24\Lib\site-packages\
error: No urls, filenames, or requirements specified (see --help)
$
```

This means Distribute is installed and is working.

We have just finished demonstrating how to install and test Distribute on Windows.

Installing Distribute on Ubuntu Linux

Ubuntu Linux does not come with the curl program pre-installed, but you can install it with:

```
$   sudo aptitude install curl
```

If you are prompted for a password, type your Ubuntu Linux account password.

Download distribute_setup.py

To download the Distribute installer, open **Applications** | **Accessories** | **Terminal** and type:

```
$ curl -O http://python-distribute.org/distribute_setup.py
```

Execute distribute_setup.py

To install Distribute, type:

```
$ python distribute_setup.py
```

You should see:

```
Installed /usr/local/lib/python2.6/dist-packages/distribute-0.6.12-py2.6.egg
Processing dependencies for distribute==0.6.12
Finished processing dependencies for distribute==0.6.12
After install bootstrap.
Creating /usr/local/lib/python2.6/dist-packages/setuptools-0.6c11-py2.6.egg-info
Creating /usr/local/lib/python2.6/dist-packages/setuptools.pth
$
```

Verify that Distribute works

To verify that Distribute works, type:

```
$ sudo easy_install
```

You should see:

```
$ sudo easy_install
install_dir /usr/local/lib/python2.6/dist-packages/
error: No urls, filenames, or requirements specified (see --help)
$
```

This means that Distribute is installed and working.

We have just finished demonstrating how to install and test Distribute on Ubuntu Linux.

Distribute comes with the **easy_install** program which you can use to install packages from the Python Package Index (http://pypi.python.org) with commands like:

```
$ easy_install package
```

Unfortunately, easy_install lacks critical features such as the ability to uninstall packages.

Fortunately, PIP (http://pip.openplans.org/) includes this feature, and more.

How to install PIP: a more user friendly Python package installer

First, let us have a look at some background on PIP.

You do not have to install PIP if you do not want to; the choice is yours. You can continue to use easy_install if you like.

 According to the Distribute propaganda, PIP works with the current Distutils library and it will work with Distutils 2, whereas the future of easy_install is uncertain.

And now we shall install PIP.

Installing PIP on Mac OS X

To install PIP, open **Finder | Applications | Utilities | Terminal** and type:

```
$ sudo easy_install pip
```

You should see:

```
Installed /Library/Python/2.6/site-packages/pip-0.7.1-py2.6.egg
Processing dependencies for pip
Finished processing dependencies for pip
$
```

To verify that PIP works, type:

```
$ sudo pip
```

You should see:

```
$ sudo pip
Usage: pip COMMAND [OPTIONS]

pip: error: You must give a command (use "pip help" see a list of commands)
$
```

We have just finished demonstrating how to install and test PIP on Ubuntu Linux.

Installing PIP on Windows 7

To install PIP, select **Start | All Programs | Accessories | Command Prompt** and type:

```
$ easy_install pip
```

You should see:

```
Installed c:\python24\lib\site-packages\pip-0.7.1-py2.4.egg
Processing dependencies for pip
Finished processing dependencies for pip
$
```

To verify that PIP works, type:

```
$ pip
```

You should see:

```
$ pip
usage: pip-script.py COMMAND [OPTIONS]

pip-script.py: error: You must give a command (use "pip help" see a list of comm
ands)

$
```

We have just finished demonstrating how to install and test PIP on Windows.

Installing PIP on Ubuntu Linux

To install PIP, open **Applications** | **Accessories** | **Terminal** and type:

```
$ sudo easy_install pip
```

You should see:

```
Installed /usr/local/lib/python2.6/dist-packages/pip-0.7.1-py2.6.egg
Processing dependencies for pip
Finished processing dependencies for pip
$
```

To verify that PIP works, type:

```
$ sudo pip
```

You should see:

```
$ sudo pip
Usage: pip COMMAND [OPTIONS]

pip: error: You must give a command (use "pip help" see a list of commands)
$
```

We have just finished demonstrating how to install and test PIP on Ubuntu Linux.

How to install Buildout—a tool for building software

First, let us have a look at some background on Buildout.

You do not have to use easy_install or PIP to install Buildout as we are about to do. Doing so will cause Buildout to be installed on your system Python's `site-packages` directory; the choice is yours.

The Zope community provides a bootstrap file for creating isolated Buildout environments outside `site-packages`: `http://svn.zope.org/repos/main/zc.buildout/trunk/bootstrap/bootstrap.py`.

If you download and execute this file, it will create a buildout in the current working directory.

We will use that method almost exclusively later, but for now, let us install Buildout globally (that is in the system Python's `site-packages` directory).

Also, let us try using PIP instead of easy_install this time (since we have just installed PIP).

Installing Buildout on Mac OS X

To install Buildout using PIP, open **Finder** | **Applications** | **Utilities** | **Terminal** and type:

```
$ sudo pip install zc.buildout
```

Namespace packages

Note that the package name of Buildout is `zc.buildout`, which indicates it is a "namespace package". To read more about this topic, visit: `http://docs.python.org/tutorial/modules.html#packages`.

You should see:

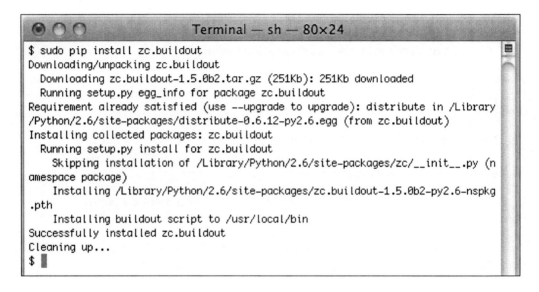

If you are prompted for a password, type your Mac OS X account password.

To verify that Buildout works, type:

```
$ buildout
```

Assuming you are not in a directory with a `buildout.cfg` file, you should see:

```
$ buildout
While:
  Initializing.
Error: Couldn't open /private/var/root/buildout.cfg
$
```

We have just finished demonstrating how to install and test Buildout on Mac OS X.

Installing Buildout on Windows 7

To install Buildout, select **Start | All Programs | Accessories | Command Prompt** and type:

```
$ pip install zc.buildout
```

You should see:

To verify that Buildout works, type:

```
$ buildout
```

We have just finished demonstrating how to install and test Buildout on Windows.

Installing Buildout on Ubuntu Linux

To install Buildout, open **Applications** | **Accessories** | **Terminal** and type:

```
$ sudo pip install zc.buildout
```

You should see:

To verify that Buildout works, type:

```
$ buildout
```

You should see:

```
$ buildout
While:
  Initializing.
Error: Couldn't open /home/aclark/buildout.cfg
$
```

We have just finished demonstrating how to install and test Buildout on Ubuntu Linux.

More about Python software distributions

At this point, we have Python 2.6 installed on both Ubuntu Linux and Mac OS X, and Python 2.4 installed on Windows. Since Plone 3.3 requires Python 2.4, we can now say we have fulfilled the Python requirement on Windows.

	Mac OS X 10.6	Windows 7	Ubuntu Linux 10.4
Python version	2.6.1	2.4.4	2.6.5
Plone 3.3 ready?	No	Almost	No

We say **No** for Mac OS X and Ubuntu Linux because we have the wrong Python version to run Plone 3.3. We say **Almost** for Windows because we have the right Python version, but no C compiler (which is required to compile Zope 2).

We have two ways to move ahead with Mac OS X and Ubuntu Linux to meet the Python 2.4 requirement:

- Install a binary distribution
- Compile from source

Binary distributions are always a good option. They save time when they are available. Unfortunately, they are not always available.

In lieu of exploring binary distributions for Mac OS X and Ubuntu Linux, we will start preparing to compile Python from source.

How to install a C compiler

Both Python and Zope 2 require a C compiler to build from source. So let us take a minute to explore the available options. Regardless of the packaging, each of the following software provides some version of the **GNU Compiler Collection (GCC)** and libraries (http://gcc.gnu.org/gcc-4.3/).

Installing a C compiler on Mac OS X

Before you can compile C code on Mac OS X, you must install **XCode** (http://developer.apple.com/technologies/tools/xcode.html).

Installing XCode

Check your Mac OS X installation DVD or Apple Developer Connection (http://developer.apple.com/) for the latest version.

Verify that GCC works

To verify that GCC works, open **Finder | Applications | Utilities | Terminal** and type:

```
$ gcc
```

You should see:

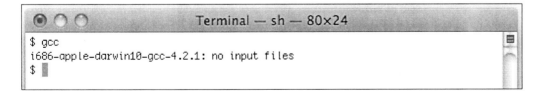

We have just finished explaining how to install and test a C compiler on Mac OS X.

Installing a C compiler on Windows

Before you can compile C code on Windows, you must install **MinGW** (or Microsoft's Visual Studio, but that approach is not covered in this book).

Downloading MinGW

To download MinGW with Internet Explorer:

1. Browse to `http://mingw.org`.
2. Click on **Downloads | View all files | Automated MinGW Installer | MinGW-5.1.6.exe**.
3. Save the file.
4. Run the installer.

Installing MinGW

Windows will present a series of dialogues you can answer based on the following suggestions:

- Select the current package
- Select **g++** and check options in addition to the base tools
- Select the default location

You should see:

Adding MinGW to the Environment Variable—Path

Now that a C compiler is installed, we would like to be able to easily run the
gcc command from the Command Prompt. To accomplish this, perform the
following steps:

1. Select **Start** | **Computer System Properties** | **Advanced system settings** |
   Environment Variables.

2. Under **System variables**, scroll down to **Path**.

3. Select **Edit**.

4. Add the following separated by a semicolon:
   - C:\MinGW\bin

5. Click on **Save**.

You should see:

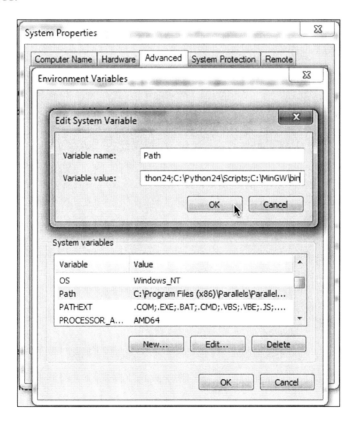

Verify that GCC works

To verify that your C compiler works, select **Start** | **All Programs** | **Accessories** | **Command Prompt** and type:

```
$ gcc
```

You should see:

```
$ gcc
gcc: no input files
$ _
```

We have just demonstrated how to install and test a C compiler on Windows.

Configuring Distutils

Later, when you try to compile Zope 2, your Buildout may fail with a Visual Studio error like this:

```
Installing zope2.
running build_ext
creating zope.proxy
copying zope/proxy\proxy.h -> zope.proxy
error: Python was built with Visual Studio 2003;
extensions must be built with a compiler than can generate compatible binaries.
Visual Studio 2003 was not found on this system. If you have Cygwin installed,
you can try compiling with MingW32, by passing "-c mingw32" to setup.py.
While:
  Installing zope2.
```

To avoid this error, you can configure Distribute to use MinGW's C compiler. Just create a file called C:\Python\Lib\Distutils\distutils.cfg, and include the following contents:

```
[build]
compiler=mingw32
```

Visit http://plone.org/documentation/kb/using-buildout-on-windows/ for more information.

Installing a C compiler on Ubuntu Linux

Before you can compile C code on Ubuntu Linux, you must install the **build-essential** package (http://packages.ubuntu.com/lucid/build-essential):

```
$ sudo aptitude install build-essential
```

You should see:

```
Setting up xz-utils (4.999.9beta+20091116-1) ...
Setting up dpkg-dev (1.15.5.6ubuntu4) ...
Setting up libstdc++6-4.4-dev (4.4.3-4ubuntu5) ...
Setting up g++-4.4 (4.4.3-4ubuntu5) ...
Setting up g++ (4:4.4.3-1ubuntu1) ...
update-alternatives: using /usr/bin/g++ to provide /usr/bin/c++ (c++) in auto mo
de.

Setting up build-essential (11.4build1) ...
Reading package lists... Done
Building dependency tree
Reading state information... Done
Reading extended state information
Initializing package states... Done
Writing extended state information... Done
$
```

Verify that GCC works

To verify that GCC works, type:

```
$ gcc
gcc: no input files
```

You should see:

```
$ gcc
gcc: no input files
$
```

We have just demonstrated how to install and test a C compiler on Ubuntu Linux.

Installing additional development libraries

Later on, when you are using Buildout to install Python, you may encounter this error:

```
Traceback (most recent call last):
  File "/home/aclark/Developer/plone-site-admin/buildout/src/python-buildout/par
ts/virtualenv/virtualenv.py", line 1129, in ?
    SITE_PY = """
LookupError: unknown encoding: zlib
```

To avoid this error, install the `zlib1g-dev` library:

```
$ sudo aptitude install zlib1g-dev
```

How to install Subversion—a version control system

The Plone community maintains several Subversion (http://subversion.apache.org/) software repositories for core and add-on software development.

In addition, the community maintains a Trac (http://trac.edgewall.org/) instance for each repository to facilitate easy browsing.

Below, you will find links to each of the Plone community's Trac instances, one for each repository:

- http://dev.plone.org/plone
- http://dev.plone.org/collective
- http://dev.plone.org/archetypes

As such, we shall make sure each of our operating systems has a Subversion client available in case we need to access software from any of the repositories.

(In the next section, we will check out a Python buildout from the **collective** repository, developed by Plone core developer Florian Schulze.)

Using Subversion on Mac OS X

Mac OS X 10.6 ships with Subversion 1.6.5 pre-installed; all we have to do is test it.

Verify that Subversion works

To verify that Subversion works, type:

```
$ svn
```

You should see:

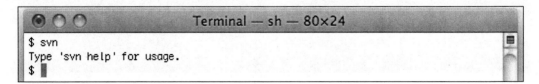

We have just demonstrated how to test Subversion on Mac OS X.

Installing Subversion on Windows

Windows 7 does not ship with Subversion pre-installed, but there is an installer available on `http://collab.net`.

Downloading Subversion

To download Subversion:

1. Create an account here: `http://www.open.collab.net/servlets/Join`.
2. Browse to `http://collab.net`. Click on **Downloads | Subversion | Windows | CollabNet Subversion Command-Line Client v1.6.9 (for Windows) | Download | Run**.
3. Run the installer.

Installing Subversion

Click on **Next**, accept the default installation location, and so on, and then wait for a few seconds.

You should see:

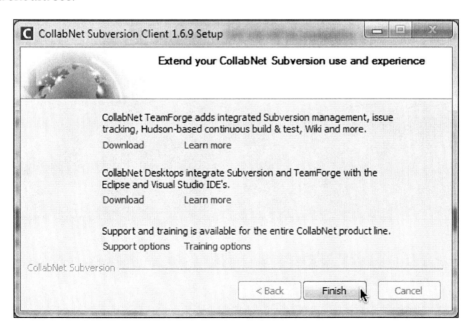

Verify that Subversion works

To verify that Subversion works, type:

```
$ svn
```

You should see:

We have just demonstrated how to install and test Subversion on Windows.

Installing Subversion on Ubuntu Linux

Ubuntu Linux does not ship with Subversion pre-installed, but you can easily install it with the following command:

```
$ sudo aptitude install subversion
```

You should see:

```
Setting up xz-utils (4.999.9beta+20091116-1) ...
Setting up dpkg-dev (1.15.5.6ubuntu4) ...
Setting up libstdc++6-4.4-dev (4.4.3-4ubuntu5) ...
Setting up g++-4.4 (4.4.3-4ubuntu5) ...
Setting up g++ (4:4.4.3-1ubuntu1) ...
update-alternatives: using /usr/bin/g++ to provide /usr/bin/c++ (c++) in auto mo
de.

Setting up build-essential (11.4build1) ...
Reading package lists... Done
Building dependency tree
Reading state information... Done
Reading extended state information
Initializing package states... Done
Writing extended state information... Done

$
```

Verify that Subversion works

To verify that Subversion works, type:

```
$ svn
```

You should see:

```
$ svn
Type 'svn help' for usage.
$
```

We have just demonstrated how to install and test Subversion on Ubuntu Linux.

How to install Python with Buildout

We have now arrived at the pinnacle task for this chapter—installing Python with Buildout.

From now on, we will not provide any operating system-specific instructions, but you can expect the examples in the rest of this book to work on all supported operating systems, unless otherwise stipulated.

Remember, we are still trying to satisfy the requirement of Python 2.4 across all the three operating systems.

Running the first buildout

In the code bundle for this chapter, you will find a file called `01-background-python.cfg`, which contains the following:

```
[buildout]
parts = python-buildout

[python-buildout]
recipe = infrae.subversion
location = src
urls = http://svn.plone.org/svn/collective/buildout/python/src/
python-buildout
```

(If you have not done so already, download the book examples from `https://www.packtpub.com/plone-3-3-site-administration/book` and unzip them into your home directory.)

Change directories to the extracted buildout directory and type:

```
$ buildout -c 01-background-python.cfg
```

You should see:

```
$ buildout -c 01-background-python.cfg

Got infrae.subversion 1.4.5.

Getting distribution for 'py'.

install_dir /Users/aclark/Developer/plone-site-admin/buildout/eggs/
tmpbIk70j

Got py 1.3.0.

/Users/aclark/Developer/plone-site-admin/buildout/eggs/infrae.subversion-
1.4.5-py2.6.egg/infrae/subversion/Common.py:4: DeprecationWarning: the
sets module is deprecated

   from sets import Set              # For python 2.3 compatibility

Installing python-buildout.
```

Running the second buildout

Inside the `buildout/src/python-buildout` directory, there is a file called `python24.cfg`.

This is the buildout that will download and build Python 2.4 for us. All we need to do is run it:

```
$ buildout -c src/python-buildout/python24.cfg
```

Early on, you may encounter an error about a missing `downloads` directory:

```
While:

   Installing python-2.4-build.

Error: The directory:

'/Users/aclark/Developer/plone-site-admin/buildout/src/python-buildout/
downloads'

to be used as a download cache doesn't exist.
```

If so, just create the directory and then re-run the `buildout` command.

You should see:

```
$ buildout -c src/python-buildout/python24.cfg

Unused options for buildout: 'base-parts'.

Updating opt.

opt: Running

...
```

```
Installing python-2.4-build.

python-2.4-build: Downloading http://www.python.org/ftp/python/2.4.6
  /Python-2.4.6.tar.bz2

python-2.4-build: Unpacking and configuring

python-2.4-build: Updating environment: CFLAGS=-arch x86_64

...

Installed /Users/aclark/Developer/plone-site-admin/buildout/src/python-
buildout/python-2.4/lib/python2.4/site-packages/PIL-1.1.6-py2.4-macosx-
10.6-i386.egg

Processing dependencies for PIL==1.1.6

Finished processing dependencies for PIL==1.1.6

Unused options for python-2.4-PIL: 'update-command'.

Installing python-2.4-test.

Unused options for python-2.4-test: 'update-script'.

$
```

Verify that Python works

To verify that Python works, type:

```
$ src/python-buildout/parts/opt/bin/python2.4
```

You should see:

```
$ src/python-buildout/parts/opt/bin/python2.4
Python 2.4.6 (#1, May  9 2010, 02:12:47)
[GCC 4.2.1 (Apple Inc. build 5659)] on darwin
Type "help", "copyright", "credits" or "license" for more information.
>>>
```

At this point, we have Python 2.4.6 installed on both Ubuntu Linux and Mac OS X, and Python 2.4.4 installed on Windows.

All of our targeted operating systems now have a version of Python capable of running Plone 3.3.

In addition, we have installed a C compiler and Subversion client.

Our computers are now ready to build Plone 3.3:

	Mac OS X 10.6	Windows 7	Ubuntu Linux 10.4
Python version	2.6.1, 2.4.6	2.4.4	2.6.5, 2.4.6
Plone 3.3 ready?	Yes	Yes	Yes

That is all for this chapter, great job! It's all downhill from here.

Summary

We have covered a lot in this chapter. To summarize, you have learned:

- Why we are here: To eliminate confusion
- What you need to get started: A computer and an operating system
- To experiment with the Plone installers—they may be all you need
- Using the system Python
- Using Python installers
- Installing Distribute, PIP, and Buildout
- Installing a C compiler and Subversion client
- Installing Python with Buildout

Remember that from now on we will not provide any instructions specific to the operating systems, but you can expect the examples in the rest of this book to work on all supported operating systems, unless otherwise stipulated.

2
Site Basics

In the previous chapter, we covered a lot of background information including how to install Python, Distribute, and PIP.

We introduced Buildout and at the end of the chapter, we saw our first Buildout configuration file.

In this chapter, we will create our first Plone site and learn how to customize its navigation and available content types.

In this chapter, you will learn:

- More about Buildout
- Adding a Plone site
- Customizing navigation
- Adding new content types

More about Buildout

According to the index page on the Python Package Index (PyPI), (`http://pypi.python.org/pypi/zc.buildout/1.5.0b2`), Buildout is a:

> *"System for managing development buildouts"*

Since its inception, Buildout has grown to become an elaborate system for building software for both development and production use. You can use it to install a single Python package or a complex application.

Buildout does very little by itself; additional functionality is provided by add-ons called recipes. And with over 200 recipes available from the PyPI, you can use it to do just about anything.

Configuration file format

Buildout's configuration file format is based on the Windows INI-style definition, described here: http://en.wikipedia.org/wiki/INI_file.

If you read the Wikipedia entry here, you will notice INI-style files are made up of parameters of the form name=value.

These parameters are separated by an equals sign (=), and can be grouped into sections of the form [section].

About the Python buildout

With that in mind, let's now analyze the configuration file 01-background-python. cfg from the previous chapter.

It looks like this:

```
[buildout]
parts = python-buildout

[python-buildout]
recipe = infrae.subversion
location = src
urls = http://svn.plone.org/svn/collective/buildout/python/src/ \
 python-buildout
```

The buildout section

A Buildout configuration file must define a buildout section:

```
[buildout]
```

The buildout section must contain a parts parameter. In the case of 01-background-python.cfg, we add the python-buildout section to the parts parameter:

```
parts = python-buildout
```

Adding parts

Parts provide a way to divide Buildout's work into logical units. Often, a recipe is used to do the actual work.

In the case of 01-background-python.cfg, we used the infrae.subversion recipe (http://pypi.python.org/pypi/infrae.subversion) to check out the Python buildout from the collective repository (http://svn.plone.org/svn/collective):

```
[python-buildout]
recipe = infrae.subversion
```

Next, we specify that we want the checkout to occur in the `src` directory (instead of the `parts` directory, which is the default) by setting the `location` parameter:

```
location = src
```

Finally, we set the value of the `urls` parameter to the following:

```
urls = http://svn.plone.org/svn/collective/buildout/python/src/ \
  python-buildout
```

This parameter's value takes two arguments, separated by a space. The first argument is the source URL, that is the checkout; the second is the target directory, that is where to put the checkout (within the `src` directory).

To learn more about this recipe's configurable parameters, read the documentation available on the Python Package Index on `http://pypi.python.org/pypi/infrae.subversion`.

Global versus local Buildout command

As you may recall, we used a "global" installation of Buildout to run the first buildout, as follows:

```
$ buildout -c 01-background-python.cfg
```

This step performs a checkout of the Python buildout, and it works because the `buildout` command is in our path.

Then we used that same "globally-installed" Buildout to run the Python buildout, as follows:

```
$ buildout -c src/python-buildout/python24.cfg
```

Now that the Python buildout is complete, we can use the resultant Python 2.4 installation for whatever we like, including bootstrapping a Plone 3.3 buildout.

Further, we do not have to use the "global" Buildout anymore, because bootstrapping will install another version of Buildout within the Plone buildout we are about to create.

So from now on, we will run the `buildout` command as:

```
$ bin/buildout
```

Introducing the Plone buildout

In the examples given in this book, you will notice two files in the
buildout directory:

- buildout.cfg
- 02-site-basics-plonesite.cfg

The buildout.cfg file contains everything you need to install Plone, assuming you
have Python 2.4 installed (which you do, if you have read Chapter 1).

It looks like this:

```
[buildout]
extends = http://dist.plone.org/release/3.3.5/versions.cfg
versions = versions
parts =
    zope2
    instance

[zope2]
recipe = plone.recipe.zope2install
url = ${versions:zope2-url}

[instance]
recipe = plone.recipe.zope2instance
zope2-location = ${zope2:location}
user = admin:admin
eggs = Plone
```

Using the extends parameter to specify versions

On the second line, you will notice an extends parameter with the following value:
http://dist.plone.org/release/3.3.5/versions.cfg.

Here, we specify that our buildout should use the section and parameter definitions
from the versions.cfg file.

One of the core features of Buildout is to be able to extend functionality from one
configuration file to another.

The versions.cfg defines a single section, called versions, with many parameters:

```
[versions]
# Buildout infrastructure
plone.recipe.zope2install = 3.2
plone.recipe.zope2instance = 3.6
plone.recipe.zope2zeoserver = 1.4
setuptools = 0.6c11
zc.buildout = 1.4.3
zc.recipe.egg = 1.2.2

# Zope
zope2-url = http://www.zope.org/Products/Zope/2.10.11/Zope-2.10.11-
final.tgz

# External dependencies
Markdown = 1.7
PIL = 1.1.6
elementtree = 1.2.7-20070827-preview
feedparser = 4.1
python-openid = 2.2.4
simplejson = 2.0.9

# Plone release
Plone = 3.3.5
Products.ATContentTypes = 1.3.4
Products.ATReferenceBrowserWidget = 2.0.5
Products.AdvancedQuery = 3.0
Products.Archetypes = 1.5.15
...
```

For most of these, the parameter name is a package name, and the value is a release number.

Next, we set the versions parameter, to ensure the versions section from versions.cfg is used in our buildout:

```
versions = versions
```

Using plone.recipe.zope2install to install Zope 2

In the `zope2` section, we use the `plone.recipe.zope2install` recipe to install Zope 2. We set the value of the `url` parameter to `${versions:zope2-url}`.

In doing so, we are using variable substitution, which is another one of Buildout's core features; you can read more about that feature on `http://pypi.python.org/pypi/zc.buildout#variable-substitutions`.

The important points are:

- The `${}` notation is used to specify a variable
- A variable consists of a section name and parameter name separated by a colon

So the `${versions:zope2-url}` variable is replaced with the value of the `zope2-url` parameter from the versions section.

Plone 4

In Plone 4, the need for a separate `zope2` section will go away!

Since Plone 4 uses Zope 2.12 and Zope 2.12 is packaged as an egg, Plone can simply list Zope 2 (the package name of Zope 2.12) as a dependency.

Using plone.recipe.zope2instance to create a Zope 2 instance

Next, in the `instance` section, we use the `plone.recipe.zope2instance` recipe to install a Zope 2 instance.

A few years ago (around the mid-2000s), it was very common to download the Zope 2 tarball (`http://www.zope.org/Products/Zope/2.10.11/Zope-2.10.11-final.tgz`) and perform the following steps by hand:

- Manually extract it and run `configure`, `make`, and `make install` to install Zope 2
- Manually create a Zope 2 instance with `mkzopeinstance.py`
- Manually install old-style products into the Zope 2 instance `Products` directory

But a few things have supplanted this technique:

- Buildout is now used to download and install Zope 2
- Buildout is now used to create instances
- Buildout is now used to add Python packages to the `sys.path`

The `plone.recipe.zope2instance` recipe requires the `zope2-location` and `user` parameters to be set.

The value of the `zope2-location` parameter is set to the (hidden) `location` parameter in the `zope2` section:

```
${zope2:location}
```

This is later substituted with the value of the Zope 2 software installation:

```
parts/zope2
```

The `user` parameter takes two arguments separated by a colon (`:`). It should be set to the Zope 2 administrator's username and password:

```
admin:admin
```

Of course, do not forget to change the password; we will get to that later. Finally, we set the value of the `eggs` parameter to `Plone`.

The PIL problem

One of the most notorious issues with running Plone is that it requires the Python Imaging Library (PIL) located at `http://www.pythonware.com/products/pil/`. If you don't have PIL installed, you don't have a working Plone site.

 Why is PIL a problem?
It is packaged in such a way that it is difficult to use with other packages.

To make using PIL with Plone easier, you can try one of these techniques: using the Python buildout, using PIP, or adding PIL to your buildout.

Using the Python buildout

As covered in Chapter 1, the Python buildout (`http://svn.plone.org/svn/collective/buildout/python/`) downloads and installs PIL for you.

Using PIP

You can use PIP to install the following version (re-packaged by core developer Hanno Schlichting): `http://dist.plone.org/thirdparty/PIL-1.1.7.tar.gz`.

This is done using the following command:

```
$ pip install http://dist.plone.org/thirdparty/PIL-1.1.7.tar.gz
```

Adding PIL to your buildout

You can add PIL to your buildout by adding the PILwoTk URL to the `find-links` parameter (in the buildout section) and the PILwoTk package name to the `eggs` parameter (in the instance section). In `pil.cfg`, we have:

```
[buildout]
extends = http://dist.plone.org/release/3.3.5/versions.cfg
versions = versions
parts =
    zope2
    instance
find-links =
    http://dist.plone.org/thirdparty/PILwoTk-1.1.6.4.tar.gz

[zope2]
recipe = plone.recipe.zope2install
url = ${versions:zope2-url}

[instance]
recipe = plone.recipe.zope2instance
zope2-location = ${zope2:location}
user = admin:admin
eggs =
    Plone
    PILwoTk
```

Now when Buildout runs, assuming you have satisfied PIL's dependencies, PIL will be installed into the buildout.

What is PILwoTk?

PILwoTk is a re-packaging of PIL by Jim Fulton of Zope Corporation. The package name is short for **PIL without Tk (PILwoTk)** and the source code has been modified to remove the Tk dependency, which Plone does not use. Because of the unique package name, using PILwoTk also avoids the possibility of downloading a potentially inoperable version of PIL from the Python Package Index.

Bootstrapping and running the buildout

In Chapter 1, we went to great lengths to install Distribute, PIP, and Buildout.

Now we will use the Python 2.4 binary we created with the Python buildout to bootstrap a Plone 3.3 buildout, except of course in Windows, where you must use the binary distribution of Python 2.4.4 that we installed (because it is not that easy to compile Python on Windows).

If you were to run the following now:

```
$ src/python-buildout/python-2.4/bin/python bootstrap.py
$ bin/buildout
```

You are likely to see a message like this from the **infrae.subversion** recipe:

```
If you sure that these modifications can be ignored, remove the
checkout manually:
   rm -rf /Users/aclark/Developer/plone-site-admin/buildout/src/python-
buildout/develop-eggs
   rm -rf /Users/aclark/Developer/plone-site-admin/buildout/src/python-
buildout/python-2.4
   rm -rf /Users/aclark/Developer/plone-site-admin/buildout/src/python-
buildout/eggs
   rm -rf /Users/aclark/Developer/plone-site-admin/buildout/src/python-
buildout/parts
   rm -rf /Users/aclark/Developer/plone-site-admin/buildout/src/python-
buildout/downloads
   rm -rf /Users/aclark/Developer/plone-site-admin/buildout/src/python-
buildout/.installed.cfg
   rm -rf /Users/aclark/Developer/plone-site-admin/buildout/src/python-
buildout/bin
...
```

To prevent this from happening, remove the, `installed.cfg` file from the root directory of the buildout:

```
$ rm .installed.cfg
```

This causes Buildout to forget about the Python Buildout. Otherwise, it would require us to remove the `src/python-buildout` directory, which we do not want to do.

Now run Buildout:

```
$ bin/buildout
```

You should see:

```
$ bin/buildout
Creating directory '/Users/aclark/Developer/plone-site-admin/buildout/
eggs'.
Getting distribution for 'plone.recipe.zope2install==3.2'.
Got plone.recipe.zope2install 3.2.
Getting distribution for 'plone.recipe.zope2instance==3.6'.
Got plone.recipe.zope2instance 3.6.
Getting distribution for 'zc.recipe.egg==1.2.2'.
Got zc.recipe.egg 1.2.2.
Uninstalling instance.
Updating zope2.
Updating fake eggs
Installing instance.
Getting distribution for 'Plone==3.3.5'.
...
Generated script '/Users/aclark/Developer/plone-site-admin/buildout/bin/
instance'.
$
```

In the output from the previous Buildout, you may notice a lot of syntax errors
of the form:

```
Installing instance.
Getting distribution for 'Plone==3.3.5'.
  File "build/bdist.macosx-10.6-i386/egg/Products/CMFPlone/skins/cmf_
legacy/TitleOrId.py", line 11
    return title
SyntaxError: 'return' outside function
  File "build/bdist.macosx-10.6-i386/egg/Products/CMFPlone/skins/plone_
content/link_redirect_view.py", line 24
    return context.REQUEST.RESPONSE.redirect(context.getRemoteUrl())
SyntaxError: 'return' outside function
File "build/bdist.macosx-10.6-i386/egg/Products/CMFPlone/skins/plone_
deprecated/cropText.py", line 9
    return context.restrictedTraverse('@@plone').cropText(text, length,
ellipsis='...')
```

You can safely ignore these.

> **Why ignore syntax errors?**
>
> The **short answer** is because they are erroneous.
>
> The **medium length answer** is because they are erroneous, and are caused by Buildout trying to install packages that contain Python scripts which are intended for use only by Zope 2.
>
> The **long answer** is that Buildout uses Distribute to install packages. During the installation process, Distribute attempts to compile the Python source code contained within the package to create Python byte code (`.py` to `.pyc`). Plone and many of its dependencies (and add-ons) contain old-style Python scripts that end with `.py` and are located inside CMF skin layer directories. Zope 2 uses these Python scripts during normal operation (for example, when a page template refers to one). However, Distribute thinks they are Python source code and tries to compile them. The compilation fails because Zope 2 does not require these scripts to have valid syntax. For example, a Python script in Zope 2 may contain `return foo`. To Python, this is a syntax error because the `return` statement is not inside a function definition, for example, `def foo():`.

Adding a Plone site

When you start Plone for the first time, there is no Plone site in the database.

Starting Plone and adding a Plone site manually

To fix the problem just mentioned, run:

```
bin/instance fg
```

You should see:

```
/Users/aclark/Developer/plone-site-admin/buildout/parts/instance/bin/
runzope -X debug-mode=on

2010-03-23 10:49:27 INFO ZServer HTTP server started at Tue Mar 23
10:49:27 2010

  Hostname: localhost

  Port: 8080

...

2010-03-23 10:49:41 INFO Zope Ready to handle requests
```

You can add a Plone site in the **Zope Management Interface (ZMI)** by following these steps:

1. Browse to `http://localhost:8080/manage`.

2. Enter the username and password specified in the `buildout.cfg` file. For example, user: **admin**, password: **admin**.

3. Add a Plone site from the **Add** menu on the upper-right.

You should see:

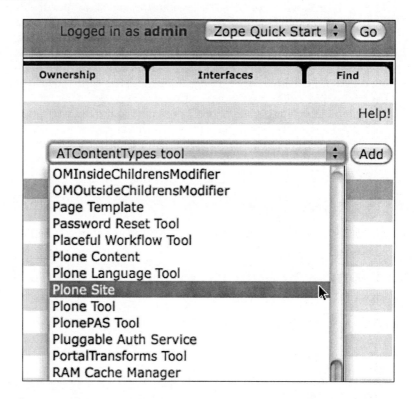

Fill in the form as follows:

- Enter **Plone** as the site **Id**
- Click on **Add Plone Site**

You should see:

Add Plone Site

Enter an ID and click the button below to create a new Plone site.

Id

Plone   (No special characters or spaces)

Title

Site

Description

Extension Profiles

You normally don't need to select anything here unless you have specific rea:

Workflow Policy Support (CMFPlacefulWorkflow)
Working Copy Support (Iterate)
OpenID Authentication Support
b-org local role plug-in
NuPlone

(Add Plone Site)

NOTE: You may only use ASCII characters for Id, Title, and Description i
outside the A-Z and numbers range are not allowed.

Now, you can browse to http://localhost:8080/Plone.

Changing the top-level Zope user's password

Now might be a good time to change the top-level Zope user's password. To do that:

1. Browse to http://localhost:8080/manage.

2. Click on **acl_users** | **users** | **Password**.

3. Type in your password in the **Password** and **Confirm password** fields, and then click on **Update Password**.

You should see:

Later, in *Chapter 7, Security*, we will discuss more things you can do to secure your site.

Adding a Plone site with Buildout

If you would like to automate the process of adding a Plone site, there is the **collective.recipe.plonesite** recipe (http://pypi.python.org/pypi/collective. recipe.plonesite).

In 02-site-basics-plonesite.cfg we have:

```
[buildout]
extends = buildout.cfg
parts += plonesite

[plonesite]
recipe = collective.recipe.plonesite
```

We extend the functionality of buildout.cfg by setting the value of the extends parameter in the buildout section to buildout.cfg.

Then we add the plonesite section by expanding the value of the parts parameter to include plonesite (by using the += syntax instead of =).

The expansion concept is an important one. It is similar to the extends parameter, which tells Buildout to include all sections and parameters from another configuration file. The += syntax tells buildout to add the new value (not replace) to the current value.

That means the parts list becomes:

- zope2
- instance
- plonesite

Now stop Plone (with *Ctrl + C* or *Ctrl + Z/ Enter*) and run:

```
$ bin/buildout -c 02-site-basics-plonesite.cfg
```

You should see:

```
$ bin/buildout -c 02-site-basics-plonesite.cfg
Getting distribution for 'collective.recipe.plonesite'.
Got collective.recipe.plonesite 1.3.
Updating zope2.
Updating fake eggs
```

```
Updating instance.
Installing plonesite.
/Users/aclark/Developer/plone-site-admin/buildout/parts/zope2/lib/python/
zope/configuration/xmlconfig.py:323: DeprecationWarning: zope.app.
annotation has moved to zope.annotation. Import of zope.app.annotation
will become unsupported in Zope 3.5
    __import__(arguments[0])
Retrieved the admin user
A Plone Site already exists and will not be replaced
```

This is because we have already added a Plone site manually. Try adding the `site-id` parameter with a different value, such as:

```
[plonesite]
recipe = collective.recipe.plonesite
site-id = Plone2
```

Now run the buildout again:

```
$ bin/buildout -c 02-site-basics-plonesite.cfg
```

You should see:

```
$ bin/buildout -c 02-site-basics-plonesite.cfg
Uninstalling plonesite.
Updating zope2.
Updating fake eggs
Updating instance.
Installing plonesite.
/Users/aclark/Developer/plone-site-admin/buildout/parts/zope2/lib/python/
zope/configuration/xmlconfig.py:323: DeprecationWarning: zope.app.
annotation has moved to zope.annotation. Import of zope.app.annotation
will become unsupported in Zope 3.5
    __import__(arguments[0])
Retrieved the admin user
/Users/aclark/Developer/plone-site-admin/buildout/eggs/Products.PlonePAS-
3.12-py2.4.egg/Products/PlonePAS/setuphandlers.py:39: DeprecationWarning:
portal_groups.getGroupIds is deprecated and will be removed in Plone 4.0.
Use PAS searchGroups instead
  existing = gtool.listGroupIds()
Added Plone Site
Quick installing: []
Running profiles: []
Finished
```

Now start Plone:

```
$ bin/instance fg
```

Browse to `http://localhost:8080/Plone2`. Alternatively, just remove the Plone site from the ZMI and run the buildout again.

To do that, browse to `http://localhost:8080/manage`, select the checkbox next to the **Plone site** object, and click on **Delete**.

You should see:

Now stop Plone (with *Ctrl + C* or *Ctrl + Z/Enter*), run Buildout, and then start Plone again:

```
$ bin/instance fg
```

You should now be able to browse to `http://localhost:8080/Plone` again.

Do not rename your Plone site object

Incidentally, even though the ZMI permits it, it's generally not a good idea to rename your Plone site. While your site may appear to work fine after a rename, there is a possibility that you may encounter an unexpected error later. This is due to the fact that the ZODB may store the object path (for example, /Plone) somewhere that will not be updated when you rename the site, among other reasons.

To read more about collective.recipe.plonesite, visit http://pypi.python.org/pypi/collective.recipe.plonesite.

Customizing site navigation

As a current Plone user, you may be familiar with Plone's automated navigation system and how to configure your global sections, navigation portlet, and sitemap.

The automated navigation system is one of the first features people notice in Plone. Create a new content item, and it will automatically appear in the global sections, navigation portlet, and sitemap. If you do not like the default behavior, you can browse to http://localhost:8080/Plone, click on **Site Setup | Navigation**, and change it.

But sometimes the default features are not enough, or there is no adjustable setting for the customization you want to perform. When this happens, you have two choices:

- Create the additional functionality yourself
- Search for the right add-on to do it for you
- Install and configure it

Regarding the first choice, you can read more about how to create additional functionality for Plone in *"Professional Plone Development"*, *Martin Aspeli*, *Packt Publishing*.

Regarding the second choice, we will discuss that here. We will now cover some add-ons that customize the navigation portlet and global sections.

Plone 3 navigation portlet extended

The **collective.portlet.sitemap** (http://pypi.python.org/pypi/collective.portlet.sitemap) package aims to enhance the functionality of the default navigation portlet by displaying more than the current level of items, similar to the way the sitemap behaves (hence the name).

To demonstrate this:

1. Browse to `http://localhost:8080/Plone` and add a folder called `Foo` to the Plone site root (using the **Add new...** menu).

2. Browse to `http://localhost:8080/Plone`. Click on **Manage Portlets | Portlets assigned here (on the left) Navigation | Start level**, set it to 0, and click on **Save**.

3. Browse to `http://localhost:8080/Plone`. You should see:

4. Browse to `http://localhost:8080/Plone`. Click on **Foo** and add a folder called **Bar**.

5. Browse to `http://localhost:8080/Plone`. Click on **Foo | Bar** and add a folder called **Baz**.

6. Browse to `http://localhost:8080/Plone`.

You should see exactly the same thing (in the navigation portlet). But with the collective.portlet.sitemap add-on installed, you would see this:

This is not to be confused with what happens when you navigate to **Baz**. With either the default navigation portlet or the collective.portlet.sitemap portlet, you would see this:

Now that we understand what the collective.portlet.sitemap add-on does, let us add it to our buildout so we can use it in Plone.

In `02-site-basics-sitemap.cfg`, we have:

```
[buildout]
extends = 02-site-basics-plonesite.cfg

[instance]
eggs += collective.portlet.sitemap
zcml += collective.portlet.sitemap
```

We extend the functionality of the previous configuration file by setting the value of the `extends` parameter (in the `buildout` section) to `02-site-basics-plonesite.cfg`.

Then we add the collective.portlet.sitemap package to the `eggs` parameter of the `instance` section.

In addition to adding the package name to the `eggs` parameter, we must add it to the `zcml` parameter, also.

Why do I have to configure Zope Configuration Markup Language (ZCML)?

The **short answer** is you do not, but in some cases you have to tell Buildout to do it for you.

The **medium length answer** is you do not, but in this case you have to tell Buildout to do it for you. This is because this package and many others do not support auto-configuration using z3c.autoinclude (http://pypi.python.org/pypi/z3c.autoinclude) yet.

As of Plone 3.3, developers and package maintainers are encouraged to spare end users from having to perform this configuration by configuring their packages to use the z3c.autoinclude entry point.

The **long answer** is that ZCML is a core feature of the Zope Component Architecture ZCA, which is mainly implemented in the zope.component (http://pypi.python.org/pypi/zope.component) and zope.interface (http://pypi.python.org/pypi/zope.interface) packages (which Plone uses with the help of the **Five** module in Zope 2).

The basic idea behind configuring ZCML is that various components of an application (Plone in this case) should be configured to work together outside the Python code. Visit http://worldcookery.com/files/ploneconf05-five/step2.html for more information.

Any add-on package that makes use of the ZCA must be configured with the help of ZCML to be used with Plone. End user exposure to this process is unfortunate, and is likely to be better hidden in future releases of Plone, as more and more add-on developers embrace the use of z3c.autoinclude. This is one big reason (but not the only reason) Buildout became a de facto standard for deploying Plone; nobody wants to manage ZCML configuration by hand.

The zcml parameter in the instance section of the buildout.cfg file creates files such as parts/instance/etc/package-includes/001-collective.portlet.sitemap.zcml, which contains ZCML markup like this:

```
<include package="collective.portlet.sitemap" file="configure.zcml" />
```

This tells Five to load the components listed in the package's configure.zcml file.

Remember that forgetting to configure ZCML in your buildout can mean the difference between a working and a (silently) non-working add-on in Plone.

Now stop Plone (with *Ctrl + C* or *Ctrl + Z/ Enter*) and run Buildout:

```
$ bin/buildout -c 02-site-basics-sitemap.cfg
```

You should see:

```
$ bin/buildout -c 02-site-basics-sitemap.cfg
Updating zope2.
Updating fake eggs
Updating instance.
Getting distribution for 'collective.portlet.sitemap'.
Got collective.portlet.sitemap 1.0.2.
```

Start Plone with:

```
$ bin/instance fg
/Users/aclark/Developer/plone-site-admin/buildout/parts/instance/bin/
runzope -X debug-mode=on
2010-03-07 18:58:34 INFO ZServer HTTP server started at Sun Mar  7
18:58:34 2010
   Hostname: localhost
   Port: 8080
...
2010-03-07 18:59:00 INFO Zope Ready to handle requests
```

Now browse to `http://localhost:8080/Plone`. Click on **Site Setup | Add-on Products**.

In the **Products available for install** section, you should see the following:

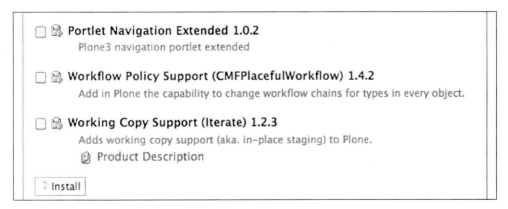

Check the box next to **Portlet Navigation Extended 1.0.2** and click on **Install**.

This will replace the default navigation portlet with the extended navigation portlet and give you the "site map in a portlet" effect.

If you click on **Manage portlets | Navigation Extended**, you will notice the extra configurable options:

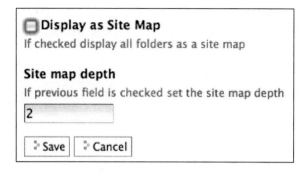

Always be prepared for the worst!

One of the most important lessons you can learn when experimenting with add-ons like this is to **never, ever, ever experiment on a production site** or a site that you care about.

Add-ons frequently don't behave as expected. They can be incomplete, inconsistent, and otherwise unreliable (and even dangerous). Hence, do not install them unless you are absolutely sure that they are going to help, and not harm your site instead.

Installing collective.portlet.explore

Another interesting add-on to explore (literally) is **collective.portlet.explore** (`http://pypi.python.org/pypi/collective.portlet.explore`).

This package enhances the default navigation portlet with JavaScript-enabled menus you can click to explore. It looks like this:

To install it, we just need to add the package name to the `eggs` and `zcml` parameters of the instance section.

We do just that in `02-site-basics-explore.cfg`, where we also extend the functionality provided by `02-site-basics-sitemap.cfg`:

```
[buildout]
extends = 02-site-basics-sitemap.cfg

[instance]
eggs += collective.portlet.explore
zcml += collective.portlet.explore
```

Now stop Plone (with *Ctrl + C* or *Ctrl + Z/ Enter*) and run Buildout:

```
$ bin/buildout -c 02-site-basics-explore.cfg
```

You should see:

```
$ bin/buildout -c 02-site-basics-explore.cfg
Uninstalling instance.
Updating zope2.
Updating fake eggs
Installing instance.
Getting distribution for 'collective.portlet.explore'.
Got collective.portlet.explore 1.0rc3.
Generated script '/Users/aclark/Developer/plone-site-admin/buildout/bin/
instance'.
```

Now start Plone:

```
$ bin/instance fg
```

Browse to `http://localhost:8080/Plone`, click on **Site Setup | Add-on Products**, and you should see:

Now, check the box next to **Explorer Portlet 1.0rc3** and click on Install.

Then browse to `http://localhost:8080/Plone`. Click on **Manage portlets** (left or right column) | **Add portlet...** | **Explorer Portlet** and click on **Save**.

Installing webcouturier.dropdownmenu

So far, we have focused only on the navigation portlet. Let us now take a look at one of the more popular add-ons to enhance the global sections (also known as portal tabs).

The fancily-named add-on **webcouturier.dropdownmenu** adds JavaScript-enabled drop-down menus to Plone's global sections.

They look like this:

Just like before, to install this add-on we need to add the package name to the `eggs` and `zcml` parameters in the `instance` section of our buildout.

We do this in `02-site-basics-dropdownmenu.cfg`, where we also extend our previous efforts in `02-site-basics-explore.cfg`:

```
[buildout]
extends = 02-site-basics-explore.cfg

[instance]
eggs += webcouturier.dropdownmenu
zcml += webcouturier.dropdownmenu
```

Now stop Plone (with *Ctrl + C* or *Ctrl + Z/Enter*) and run Buildout:

```
$ bin/buildout -c 02-site-basics-dropdownmenu.cfg
Uninstalling instance.
Updating zope2.
Updating fake eggs
Installing instance.
Getting distribution for 'webcouturier.dropdownmenu'.
Got webcouturier.dropdownmenu 2.0.
Generated script '/Users/aclark/Developer/plone-site-admin/buildout/bin/
instance'.
```

Start Plone:

```
$ bin/instance fg
```

Browse to `http://localhost:8080/Plone`. Click on **Site Setup | Add-on Products** and you should see:

Check the box next to **Dropdown menu 2.0** and click on **Install**.

After that, your global sections should "drop down" if they contain sub-items, for example, folders, pages, and so on.

We have now covered three examples of how to add and configure add-ons to enhance Plone's navigation features.

You can find and experiment with more add-ons at the Python Package Index (PyPI) (`http://pypi.python.org/pypi`). You can also visit `http://plone.org` and click on **Downloads** (`http://plone.org/products`).

While a search for **navigation** on PyPI turns up some useful results, it is somewhat of a mixed bag because it contains plenty of non-Plone results as well:

Index of Packages Matching 'navigation'

Not Logged In
Login
Register
Lost Login?
Use OpenID
lp

Package	Score	Description
collective.facetednavigation 0.7.2	9	Collective Faceted Navigation provides an user interface which lets an user browse items of a Plone site by selecting amongst pre-defined criteria.
collective.navigationtoggle 0.2.0	9	Make possible to expand/collapse specific Plone navigation entries in a very unobtrusive way
zamplugin.navigation 0.5.0	9	Navigation for ZAM Zope 3 Application Management

On the other hand, a **plone.org** search is guaranteed to have all Plone-specific results:

One thing is for certain—there are seemingly endless amount of options to explore and you are encouraged to do so.

Adding new content types

You may be familiar with Plone's content types and how to add content to your site. If not, please read Chapters 4, 5, and 6 of "*Practical Plone 3*", *Veda Williams, Packt Publishing* where this subject is covered in detail.

Often, it is necessary to add additional content types to provide a particular functionality. This is not to say adding a new content type is always a good idea, but some problems are particularly well-suited to being solved with the addition of a new content type.

Adding a blog entry type

For example, some folks like to blog with Plone. One of the simplest ways to start blogging with Plone is to use the Scrawl add-on (**Products.Scrawl** package), which creates a new blog content type (by copying the news item content type):

You can easily add the Scrawl add-on as follows. In `02-site-basics-blog.cfg`, we have:

```
[buildout]
extends = 02-site-basics-dropdownmenu.cfg

[instance]
eggs += Products.Scrawl
```

Now stop Plone (with *Ctrl + C* or *Ctrl + Z*/ *Enter*) and run Buildout:

```
$ bin/buildout -c 02-site-basics-blog.cfg
```

You should see:

```
$ bin/buildout -c 02-site-basics-blog.cfg
Uninstalling plonesite.
Uninstalling instance.
Updating zope2.
Updating fake eggs
Installing instance.
Getting distribution for 'Products.Scrawl'.
Got Products.Scrawl 1.3.2.
Generated script '/Users/aclark/Developer/plone-site-admin/buildout/bin/
instance'.
```

Now start Plone:

```
$ bin/instance fg
```

Browse to `http://localhost:8080/Plone Site Setup` and click on **Add/Remove Products**.

In the **Products available for install** section, you should see:

Check the box next to **Scrawl 1.3.2** and click on **Install**.

Browse to `http://localhost:8080/Plone` and create a new **Blog Entry**:

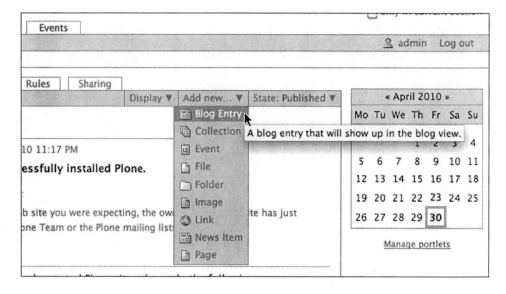

Fill in the **Title** field and click on **Save**.

You should see:

If you browse to `http://localhost:8080/Plone`, you will notice that your Plone site still looks the same. Certainly, it does not look like a blog. Two things will fix that for us:

- Configure the Plone site to display the **Blog view** template provided by Scrawl
- Use the syndication feature provided by Plone to create a syndicated feed of our blog entries

Configure the blog_view

To enable the blog view on the home page, we will have to:

- Know the name of the template
- Configure it as an available view for the Plone site content type

We can find out the name of the template by navigating to the **News** folder and selecting the **Display** menu.

You should see:

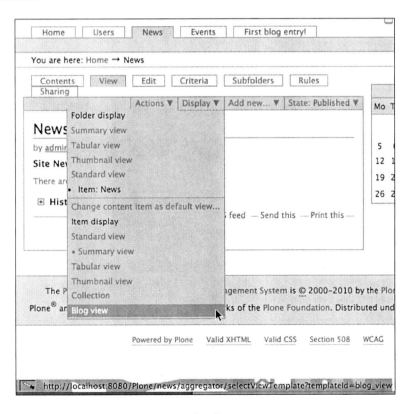

Notice that at the very bottom of the browser in the status bar, the name of the **Blog view** template is **blog_view**.

We can add **blog_view** to the Plone site's available views like this:

1. Browse to `http://localhost:8080/Plone`. Click on **Site Setup | Zope Management Interface | portal_types | Plone Site | Available views**.

2. Add **blog_view** to the list of **Available view methods** and click on **Save Changes**.

You should see:

Once that is done, select **Blog view** from the **View** menu on the Plone site, like this:

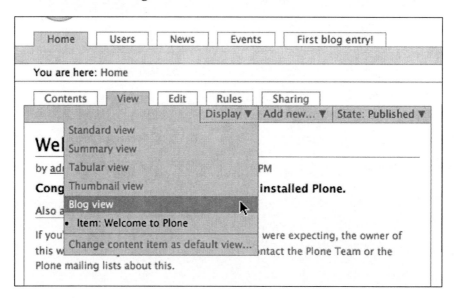

Configure the RSS feed

Now, let us enable syndication on the Plone site object.

One of the attractive features of Plone is its ability to syndicate content (that is, create an RSS feed). This feature is enabled by default on the news items and events folders. Unfortunately, the ability to configure syndication for other types of content is disabled by default.

To re-enable it, let's re-enable the link to the configuration form in the Plone user interface. Navigate to **Site Setup** | **Zope Management Interface** | **portal_actions** | **object** | **Syndication** | **Visible**.

Check the **Visible** box and click on **Save Changes**.

You should see:

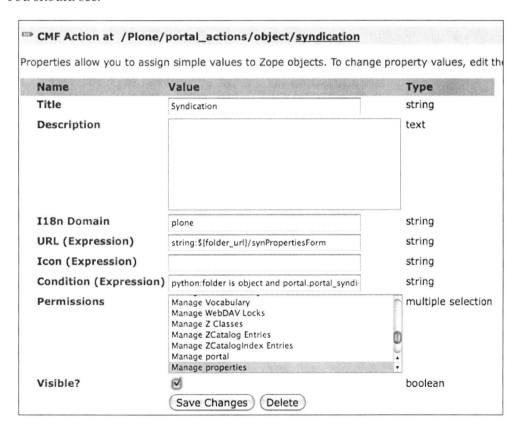

Now return to the Plone site, navigate to **Contents | Syndication | Syndication Properties | Enable syndication**, and click on it.

Adjust the default settings if you like, and click on **Save Changes**.

Now if you return to the Plone site, you should see the following at the bottom:

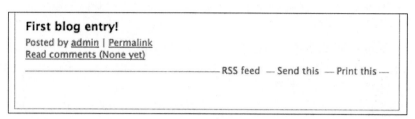

Of course, there is other content in this folder, which you can either delete or set to the private state so that it is not seen by the public.

If you click on the RSS feed link, you'll see that Plone is generating an RSS feed that your browser will be happy to consume:

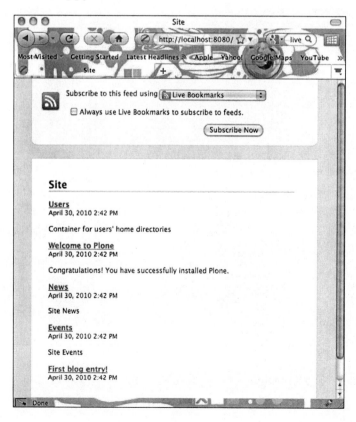

Plone 4

In Plone 4, there will be a blog view included! That means any content item can be a blog entry.

In the most common scenario, you will configure the blog view to be the default view for a collection. The collection will display the items you configure to be blog entries, for example, pages.

Visit core developer David Glick's website at http://davisagli. com/ in order to see the Plone 4 blog view in action (thanks to the creator, Laurence Rowe).

Summary

That's it for this chapter. You have done another impressive amount of work, congratulations!

You have learned:

- How Buildout configuration files work
- How to add a Plone site with Buildout
- How to customize navigation in Plone with add-ons
- How to create a weblog with Plone using the Scrawl add-on

In the next chapter, we will learn how to use Buildout to install new themes.

3
Appearance

Soon after you install and run Plone for the first time, you will probably want to change the appearance. The effort needed to do so varies, and depends largely on your goals. If you are not picky, adding a new theme to Plone can be as simple as adding a package to your `buildout.cfg` file, running Buildout, and restarting Plone.

However, if you want a high quality, unique, and a professional-looking theme for your site, it could take several days, weeks, or even months to achieve the desired result.

In this chapter, we will cover the spectrum from easy and small changes with a high impact to more complex changes that require more effort. However, keep in mind that this is not a comprehensive coverage, help is just enough to rather a site administrator gain speed quickly. If you want to learn theming in depth, see the book *"Plone 3 Theming"*, *Veda Williams*, *Packt Publishing*.

In this chapter, you will learn:

- Installing themes with Buildout
- Examining themes with **Omelette** and Python
- Overview of theme package files
- Creating a theme package with **ZopeSkel**
- Examining themes in the ZMI
- Making changes through the Web

Installing themes with Buildout

For a lot of website projects, a theme downloaded from plone.org (`http://plone.org/products`) or the Python Package Index (`http://pypi.python.org`) is enough to launch a professional-looking site. If your project falls into this category, or if you just want to experiment, follow the steps in this chapter.

Searching for themes on plone.org

We will need to find a theme we like. We can do that by browsing to `http://plone.org`. Next, click on **Downloads | Add-on Product Releases | Themes**.

You should see (result similar to):

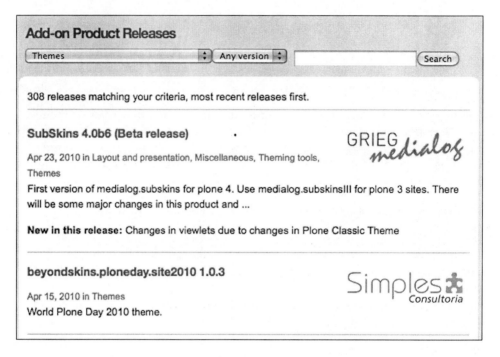

Click on a theme to view a screenshot and select one you like, for example **beyondskins.ploneday.site2010**, and add the package to your `buildout.cfg` file.

Adding themes with Buildout

In `03-appearance-wpd2010.cfg`, we extend the last known working configuration file from Chapter 2, that is `02-site-basics-blog.cfg`.

It looks like this:

```
[buildout]
extends = 02-site-basics-blog.cfg

[instance]
eggs += beyondskins.ploneday.site2010
zcml += beyondskins.ploneday.site2010
```

In addition to adding the package name to the eggs parameter, we must add it to the zcml parameter as well.

Refer to *Chapter 2, Site Basics,* for a detailed explanation of why this is necessary.

Now stop Plone (with *Ctrl + C* or *Ctrl +Z/ Enter*) and run:

```
$ bin/buildout -c 03-appearance.cfg
Updating zope2.
Updating fake eggs
Updating instance.
Getting distribution for 'beyondskins.ploneday.site2010'.
Got beyondskins.ploneday.site2010 1.0.3.
```

Now start Plone:

```
$ bin/instance fg
```

Installing themes in Plone

Browse to http://localhost:8080/Plone. Now, click on **Site Setup | Add/ Remove Products** and you should see:

Check the box next to **WorldPloneDay: Theme for 2010 edition 1.0.3** and click on **Install**.

Now browse to http://localhost:8080/Plone and you should see:

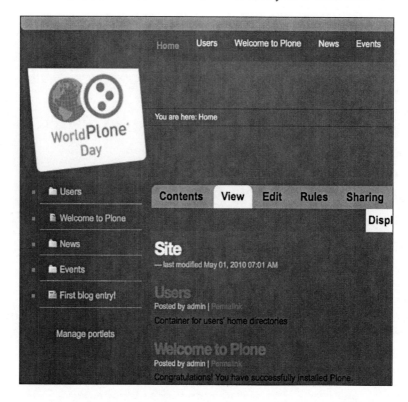

 This theme is the courtesy of **Simples Consultoria** (http://www.simplesconsultoria.com.br/). Thank you!

You can examine the anonymous view (what everyone else sees) by loading http://127.0.0.1:8080/Plone in your browser (that is. by using the IP address instead of the hostname). You can also load either of these URLs (http://127.0.0.1:8080/Plone or http://localhost:8080/Plone) from another web browser (besides the one you are currently using) to see the anonymous view (for example, Safari or Internet Explorer, instead of Firefox).

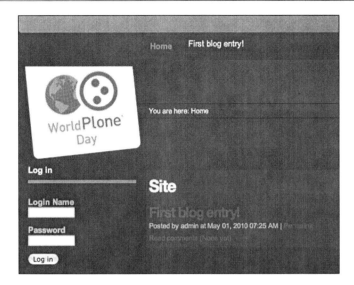

To display the blog entry we created in Chapter 2 to the public, we have transitioned the other objects in the site root to the private state.

If you are unfamiliar with how to transition objects from the public state to the private state, please see Chapter 9 of *"Practical Plone 3"*, *Veda Williams*, *Packt Publishing*.

Examining themes with Omelette and Python

Simply put, a theme is a collection of templates, images, CSS, JavaScript, and other files (such as Python scripts) that control the appearance of your site.

Typically these files are packaged into a Python package, installed in your Plone site with the help of Buildout, and installed in Plone via the **Add/Remove Products** configlet in **Site Setup**.

Once installed, certain elements of the theme can be edited through the Web using the ZMI. However, these changes only exist in the site's database. Currently there is no easy way to transfer changes made through the Web from the database to the filesystem; so there is a trade-off for performing such customizations through the Web. If you lose your database, you lose your customizations.

Depending on your goals, it may not be entirely undesirable to store customizations in your database. But nowadays, most folks choose to separate their site's logical elements (for example themes, add-on functionality, and so on) from their site's content (that is data).

Creating a filesystem theme and resisting the urge to customize it through the Web accomplishes this goal. Otherwise, if you are going to customize your theme through the Web, consider these changes volatile, and subject to loss.

Installing and using Omelette

A great way to examine files on the filesystem is to add Omelette (http://pypi. python.org/pypi/collective.recipe.omelette) to your buildout.cfg and examine the files in the parts/omelette directory.

Omelette is a Buildout recipe that creates (UNIX filesystem) symbolic links from all the Zope 2, Plone, and add-on installation files to one convenient location. This makes the job of examining files on the filesystem much easier.

To install Omelette, in 03-appearance-omelette.cfg, we have this:

```
[buildout]
extends = 03-appearance-wpd2010.cfg
parts +=
    omelette

[omelette]
recipe = collective.recipe.omelette
eggs = ${instance:eggs}
packages = ${zope2:location}/lib/python
```

In this configuration file, we extend the sections and parameters in 03-appearance-wpd2010.cfg, and add a new section called omelette to the parts parameter (in the buildout section).

Remember that using the += syntax adds the new value to the current value, so the parts list becomes:

```
parts = zope2 instance plonesite omelette
```

(We can examine the current state of the buildout by looking in the .installed.cfg file in the root directory of the buildout.)

We also tell Omelette what files to link in the eggs and packages parameters:

- ${instance:eggs}: Refers to the packages in the eggs directory.
- ${zope2:location}/lib/python: Refers to the modules in the parts/zope2/lib/python/ directory.

You can read more about how to configure Omelette here: http://pypi.python. org/pypi/collective.recipe.omelette.

Now stop Plone (with *Ctrl* + *C* or *Ctrl* +*Z*/*Enter*) and run:

```
$ bin/buildout -c 03-appearance-omelette.cfg
```

You should see:

```
$ bin/buildout -c 03-appearance-omelette.cfg

Getting distribution for 'collective.recipe.omelette'.

Got collective.recipe.omelette 0.9.

Uninstalling plonesite.

Updating zope2.

Updating fake eggs

Updating instance.

Installing plonesite.
/Users/aclark/Developer/plone-site-admin/buildout/parts/zope2/lib/python/
zope/configuration/xmlconfig.py:323: DeprecationWarning: zope.app.
annotation has moved to zope.annotation. Import of zope.app.annotation
will become unsupported in Zope 3.5

    __import__(arguments[0])

Retrieved the admin user

A Plone Site already exists and will not be replaced

Installing omelette.
```

> **Omelette in Windows**
>
> As of version 0.5, Windows supports Omelette if you have the **Junction** program installed (and configured in your path). Junction is easy to install, and available here: `http://www.microsoft.com/technet/sysinternals/fileanddisk/junction.mspx`.

Now that Omelette has been installed, take a look in the `parts/omelette` directory. You should see:

```
$ ls -1 parts/omelette

Products/

archetypes/

beyondskins/

borg/

collective/

easy_install.py@

elementtree@
```

```
feedparser.py@
five/
kss/
markdown.py@
mdx_footnotes.py@
mdx_rss.py@
openid@
pkg_resources.py@
plone/
setuptools@
simplejson@
site.py@
webcouturier/
wicked/
z3c/
zc/
```

Exploring modules with zopepy

These files correspond directly to the modules available in Python when Plone is running. To demonstrate this, let us configure a Python interpreter with the modules added to the sys.path.

In 03-appearance-zopepy.cfg, we have this:

```
[buildout]
extends = 03-appearance-omelette.cfg
parts +=
    zopepy

[zopepy]
recipe = zc.recipe.egg
eggs = ${instance:eggs}
interpreter = zopepy
extra-paths = ${zope2:location}/lib/python
scripts = zopepy
```

We extend the last working configuration in 03-appearance-omelette.cfg and add a new section called zopepy (short for "Zope Python").

Now stop Plone (with *Ctrl + C* or *Ctrl +Z/ Enter*) and run Buildout:

```
$ bin/buildout -c 03-appearance-zopepy.cfg
```

You should see:

```
$ bin/buildout -c 03-appearance-zopepy.cfg
Uninstalling plonesite.
Updating zope2.
Updating fake eggs
Updating instance.
Installing plonesite.
/Users/aclark/Developer/plone-site-admin/buildout/parts/zope2/lib/python/
zope/configuration/xmlconfig.py:323: DeprecationWarning: zope.app.
annotation has moved to zope.annotation. Import of zope.app.annotation
will become unsupported in Zope 3.5
    __import__(arguments[0])
Retrieved the admin user
A Plone Site already exists and will not be replaced
Updating omelette.
The recipe for omelette doesn't define an update method. Using its
install method.
Installing zopepy.
Generated interpreter '/Users/aclark/Developer/plone-site-admin/buildout/
bin/zopepy'.
```

This creates a script that invokes the Python interpreter with the Plone modules added to the sys.path. Now if you run bin/zopepy, you can explore modules in Python.

For example, you can import the beyondskins module (from the top-level namespace):

```
$ bin/zopepy
>>> import beyondskins
>>>
```

Python will try to evaluate any statement you input. For example, type beyondskins and hit *Enter*:

```
>>> beyondskins
<module 'beyondskins' from '/Users/aclark/Developer/plone-site-
admin/buildout/eggs/beyondskins.ploneday.site2010-1.0.3-py2.4.egg/
beyondskins/__init__.pyc'>
```

Python will tell you that beyondskins is a module. You can also try to call beyondskins (as if it were a function or class method):

```
>>> beyondskins()
Traceback (most recent call last):
  File "<console>", line 1, in ?
TypeError: 'module' object is not callable
```

Python will now tell you that module objects are not callable. You can use the built-in `dir` function to view the attributes of the beyondskins module:

```
>>> dir(beyondskins)
['__builtins__', '__doc__', '__file__', '__name__', '__path__',
'ploneday']
```

Now, Python will tell you its attributes. You can inquire about a specific attribute such as __path__:

```
>>> beyondskins.__path__
['/Users/aclark/Developer/plone-site-admin/buildout/eggs/beyondskins.
ploneday.site2010-1.0.3-py2.4.egg/beyondskins']
>>>
```

Python will return its value. Just for fun, you can inquire about any attribute of any module:

```
>>> Products.__path__
['/Users/aclark/Developer/plone-site-admin/buildout/eggs/Plone-3.3.5-
py2.4.egg/Products',
...
```

The value of `Products.__path__` is too long to print here. It contains a list of all packages that contain a Products module. All of this code ends up in the Products namespace in Python, handy!

We could spend the rest of the book learning Python, but let's return to theming instead.

Overview of theme package files

You will notice a `beyondskins` directory in `parts/omelette` that contains two files:

- `__init__.py`
- `ploneday`

The `__init__.py` file tells Python to treat this directory as a module, and that `ploneday` is another directory.

Plone packages typically do not make use of the top-level or mid-level namespaces, so let us look inside (the third-level module) `beyondskins/ploneday/site2010` instead:

```
$ ls -H -1 parts/omelette/beyondskins/ploneday/site2010
README.txt
__init__.py
__init__.pyc
__init__.pyo
browser/
configure.zcml
doc/
locales/
profiles/
profiles.zcml
setuphandlers.py
setuphandlers.pyc
setuphandlers.pyo
skins/
skins.zcml
tests.py
tests.pyc
tests.pyo
updateTranslations.sh
version.txt
```

Here is an overview of (most of) these files and directories:

- `__init__.py`: This file tells Python the directory is a module; see `http://docs.python.org/tutorial/modules.html` for more information.

- `__init.__pyc`: This file contains compiled byte code; see `http://docs.python.org/tutorial/modules.html` for more information.

- `__init__.pyo`: This file contains optimized and compiled byte code; see `http://docs.python.org/tutorial/modules.html` for more information.

- `browser/`: This directory contains new-style customization code (that is, code that makes use of the Zope Component Architecture), such as browser views, portlets, viewlets, and resources like image, CSS, and JavaScript files. Visit: `http://plone.org/documentation/kb/customization-for-developers/zope-3-browser-views` for more information.

- `configure.zcml`: This file contains ZCML code used to load components defined in your package. It is also responsible for loading other ZCML files within a package:

```
<include package=".browser" />
<include file="skins.zcml" />
<include file="profiles.zcml" />
```

- `locales/`: This directory contains translations for multilingual sites. Visit `http://plone.org/documentation/manual/developer-manual/internationalization-i18n-and-localization-l10n` for more information.

- `profiles/`: This directory contains **GenericSetup** (`http://plone.org/documentation/kb/genericsetup`) code typically in the default directory, to indicate the default profile. GenericSetup can be used to configure all manner of settings in Plone. If you are not familiar with it, try the following:

  - Navigate to **Site Setup | Zope Management Interface | portal_setup | Export**
  - Scroll to the bottom and click on **Export all steps**

- You will get a compressed, archived file that contains many XML files containing various settings. You can add these files to the `profiles/default/` directory of your add-on package, then edit them to customize the settings.

- `setuphandlers.py`: While many settings can be configured using GenericSetup, some cannot. This file holds ad hoc Python code used to configure various settings that cannot be configured elsewhere (that is, using GenericSetup). For more information about `setuphandlers.py`, see Chapter 6 of *"Professional Plone Development"*, *Martin Aspeli, Packt Publishing*.

- `skins/`: This directory contains Zope 2 **File System Directory Views (FSDV)** that contain **Content Management Framework (CMF)** skin layers that contain templates, images, CSS/JavaScript files, and Python scripts.

- `skins.zcml/`: This file contains ZCML code that registers FSDVs used by the CMF to facilitate skin layers.

```
<configure
    xmlns="http://namespaces.zope.org/zope"
    xmlns:cmf="http://namespaces.zope.org/cmf"
    i18n_domain="beyondskins.ploneday.site2010">

  <!-- File System Directory Views registration -->
  <cmf:registerDirectory
      name="beyondskins_ploneday_site2010_images"/>
  <cmf:registerDirectory
      name="beyondskins_ploneday_site2010_templates"/>
  <cmf:registerDirectory
      name="beyondskins_ploneday_site2010_styles"/>

  <!-- Note: This could also be done for all folders at once
       by replacing the previous lines with this one:
  <cmf:registerDirectory name="skins" directory="skins"
      recursive="True" />
  -->

</configure>
```

- `tests.py`: This file (or directory) typically contains unit tests (and doctests) for the package. See `http://plone.org/documentation/kb/testing` for more information.

Creating a theme package with ZopeSkel

Now that we have examined someone else's theme, let us try creating our own.

Remember, we will not cover theme creation in depth; this is only a sample for site administrators (who may or may not be required to develop themes, in addition to managing their site).

For more information about creating themes, Visit: http://plone.org/ documentation/kb/how-to-create-a-plone-3-theme-product-on-the-filesystem, or Chapter 4 of "*Plone 3 Theming*", *Veda Williams, Packt Publishing.*

To create a theme, we will use the ZopeSkel tool (http://pypi.python.org/pypi/ ZopeSkel) to generate some of the boilerplate code. ZopeSkel uses **PasteScript** (http://pypi.python.org/pypi/PasteScript) to facilitate package generation using a set of templates.

Other options include:

- Write everything by hand from memory
- Copy the contents of another theme package
- Use another tool such as ArchGenXML to generate boilerplate code (http://plone.org/products/archgenxml)

Adding ZopeSkel to a buildout

Now let's add ZopeSkel to our buildout.

In 03-appearance-zopeskel.cfg, we have this:

```
[buildout]
extends = 03-appearance-zopepy.cfg
parts +=
    zopeskel

[zopeskel]
recipe = zc.recipe.egg
dependent-scripts = true
```

We extend the previous working configuration file, and add a new section called zopeskel.

This section uses the zc.recipe.egg recipe (http://pypi.python.org/pypi/ zc.recipe.egg) to download ZopeSkel from the Python Package Index (zc.recipe.egg will search the Python Package Index for packages that match the section name zopeskel).

We set `dependent-scripts` to true, to tell Buildout to generate Python scripts for ZopeSkel's dependencies such as PasteScript, which includes the `paster` script.

Now stop Plone (with *Ctrl + C* or *Ctrl + Z/ Enter*) and run Buildout:

```
$ bin/buildout -c 03-appearance-zopeskel.cfg
```

You should see:

```
$ bin/buildout -c 03-appearance-zopeskel.cfg
Uninstalling plonesite.
Updating zope2.
Updating fake eggs
Updating instance.
Installing plonesite.
...
Updating zopepy.
Installing zopeskel.
Getting distribution for 'zopeskel'.
Got ZopeSkel 2.16.
Getting distribution for 'Cheetah>1.0,<=2.2.1'.
...
Got Cheetah 2.2.1.
Getting distribution for 'PasteScript'.
Got PasteScript 1.7.3.
Getting distribution for 'PasteDeploy'.
...
Got PasteDeploy 1.3.3.
Getting distribution for 'Paste>=1.3'.
...
Got Paste 1.7.3.1.
Generated script '/Users/aclark/Developer/plone-site-admin/buildout/bin/
zopeskel'.
Generated script '/Users/aclark/Developer/plone-site-admin/buildout/bin/
paster'.
Generated script '/Users/aclark/Developer/plone-site-admin/buildout/bin/
easy_install'.
Generated script '/Users/aclark/Developer/plone-site-admin/buildout/bin/
easy_install-2.4'.
```

You will notice that in addition to `bin/zopeskel`, Buildout also installed the "dependent scripts" `bin/paster` and `bin/easy_install` (the latter of which we do not really need in this case).

Running ZopeSkel

Now try running ZopeSkel with the command:

`$ bin/zopeskel`

You should see:

```
Usage:

    zopeskel <template> <output-name> [var1=value] ... [varN=value]

    zopeskel --help              Full help
    zopeskel --list              List template verbosely, with details
    zopeskel --make-config-file  Output .zopeskel prefs file
...
```

This tells us we need to pick a template and output-name.

ZopeSkel goes on to list the available templates. They are:

```
archetype:          A Plone project that uses Archetypes content types
kss_plugin:         A project for a KSS plugin
plone:              A project for Plone products
plone2_theme:       A theme for Plone 2.1
plone3_portlet:     A Plone 3 portlet
plone_app:          A project for Plone products with a nested namespace
plone_pas:          A project for a Plone PAS plugin
plone2.5_theme:     A theme for Plone 2.5
plone3_theme:       A theme for Plone 3
plone2.5_buildout:  A buildout for Plone 2.5 projects
plone3_buildout:    A buildout for Plone 3 installation
plone_hosting:      Plone hosting: buildout with ZEO and Plone
recipe:             A recipe project for zc.buildout
silva_buildout:     A buildout for Silva projects
```

```
basic_namespace:    A basic Python project with a namespace package
nested_namespace:   A basic Python project with a nested
basic_zope:         A Zope project
```

In our case, we will choose `plone3_theme`.

The output-name is the name of the package we want to create for example, `my.theme`.

Since we are creating a new package, let us change directories to the `src` directory and run ZopeSkel from there, like this:

```
$ cd src
$ ../bin/zopeskel plone3_theme my.theme
```

You should see:

```
$ ../bin/zopeskel plone3_theme my.theme
plone3_theme: A theme for Plone 3

This creates a project for a theme for Plone 3.
...
```

This will be followed by a series of questions, which you can answer based on these suggestions:

- **Mode: Easy**: This mode asks the least number of questions it needs to do its job.
- **Skin name: My Theme**: This name will show up in various places, including **Site Setup | Add/Remove Products**.
- **Empty styles: False**: This means we want our theme to look like the Plone Default theme. If you answer True, you will get an unstyled theme instead.
- **Include documentation: True**: This means our code will be generated with helpful comments included inline.
- **Version: 1.0**: This means our theme is ready for production use! Feel free to adjust this value if you like.
- **Description: An installable theme for Plone 3**: You can change this to whatever you like.

Running Paster

Next, when ZopeSkel completes, it tells us about the additional commands we can run to generate more boilerplate code.

We do not need to do it now, but if you are curious, try this:

```
$ cd my.theme
$ ../../bin/paster addcontent --list-all
```

You should see the following templates available (to generate more boilerplate code):

```
anonymous_user_factory_plugin:    A Plone PAS AnonymousUserFactory Plugin
atschema:                         A handy AT schema builder
authentication_plugin:            A Plone PAS Authentication Plugin
challenge_plugin:                 A Plone PAS Challenge Plugin
contenttype:                      A content type skeleton
credentials_reset_plugin:         A Plone PAS CredentialsReset Plugin
extraction_plugin:                A Plone PAS Extraction Plugin
form:                             A form skeleton
formfield:                        Schema field for a form
group_enumeration_plugin:         A Plone PAS GroupEnumeration Plugin
groups_plugin:                    A Plone PAS Groups Plugin
i18nlocale:                       An i18n locale directory structure
portlet:                          A Plone 3 portlet
properties_plugin:                A Plone PAS Properties Plugin
role_assigner_plugin:             A Plone PAS RoleAssigner Plugin
role_enumeration_plugin:          A Plone PAS RoleEnumeration Plugin
roles_plugin:                     A Plone PAS Roles Plugin
update_plugin:                    A Plone PAS Update Plugin
user_adder_plugin:                A Plone PAS UserAdder Plugin
user_enumeration_plugin:          A Plone PAS UserEnumeration Plugin
user_factory_plugin:              A Plone PAS UserFactory Plugin
validation_plugin:                A Plone PAS Validation Plugin
view:                             A browser view skeleton
zcmlmeta:                         A ZCML meta directive skeleton
```

Some of these which apply to themes are:

- i18nlocale
- portlet
- view

To add a portlet (little boxes on the left and right side of your site) to your theme, try this:

```
$ ../../bin/paster addcontent portlet
```

We could go on, but let's come back to basics now.

We now have a new theme package, but we do not have a new theme package in our buildout or in Plone. Let us now add our package to the buildout and to Plone.

The easiest way to do this is to tell Buildout we are developing a new package, by setting the value of the `develop` parameter in the `buildout` section to our package name (and relative filesystem path, in this case `src/my.theme`).

In addition to making Plone aware of this package, we must list it in the `eggs` parameter of the `instance` section.

In `03-appearance-develop.cfg`, we have:

```
[buildout]
extends = 03-appearance-zopeskel.cfg
develop = src/my.theme

[instance]
eggs += my.theme
```

Now stop Plone (with *Ctrl + C* or *Ctrl + Z/Enter*) and run Buildout:

```
$ bin/buildout -c 03-appearance-develop.cfg
```

You should see:

```
$ bin/buildout -c 03-appearance-develop.cfg
Develop: '/Users/aclark/Developer/plone-site-admin/buildout/src/my.theme'
Uninstalling plonesite.
Updating zope2.
Updating fake eggs
Updating instance.
Installing plonesite.
...
```

The first line indicates that Buildout has recognized our new package. You may encounter an error during the Buildout run, when the `collective.recipe.plonesite` recipe tries to start Plone and add a Plone site. Ignore that for now. In fact when Buildout finishes and you restart Zope, you may see an (obnoxiously long) error like this:

```
$ bin/instance fg
/Users/aclark/Developer/plone-site-admin/buildout/parts/instance/bin/
runzope -X debug-mode=on
2010-05-02 11:38:08 INFO ZServer HTTP server started at Sun May  2
11:38:08 2010

...

    OSError: [Errno 2] No such file or directory: '/Users/aclark/
Developer/plone-site-admin/buildout/my.theme/my/theme/locales'
```

But this error is good; it means we have succeeded in adding our package to Buildout and Plone.

To fix this error (if you get it), create a `locales` directory where Plone says one is needed (ZopeSkel forgot to do this for us; a future release that is a release newer than ZopeSkel 2.16 should address the problem.):

```
$ mkdir src/my.theme/my/theme/locales
```

Now start Plone and you should see:

```
$ bin/instance fg
/Users/aclark/Developer/plone-site-admin/buildout/parts/instance/bin/
runzope -X debug-mode=on
2010-05-02 11:44:28 INFO ZServer HTTP server started at Sun May  2
11:44:28 2010
        Hostname: 0.0.0.0
        Port: 8080

...

2010-05-02 11:44:40 INFO Application New disk product detected,
determining if we need to fix up any ZClasses.
2010-05-02 11:44:40 INFO Zope Ready to handle requests
```

The second to last line indicates that Zope 2 has found our package!

Next, browse to `http://localhost:8080/Plone`. Now, click on **Site Setup | Add/Remove Products** and look for our package in the Quick Installer:

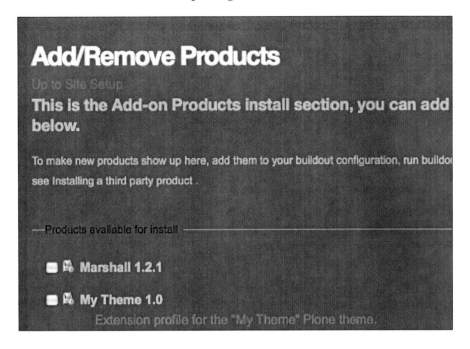

Check the box next to **My Theme 1.0** and click **Install**.

You will notice the beyondskins.ploneday.site2010 theme has disappeared, and the Plone Default theme has returned (because My Theme 1.0 is based on Plone Default).

Now that our theme is installed, we can try to make a simple customization, like changing the logo.

To do that, we are going to copy a file with the same name as the default logo to our custom images directory: `src/my/theme/skins/my_theme_custom_images`.

But how do we know the logo image filename? One easy way to find it is to use the Firefox web browser with the Firebug add-on installed (`http://getfirebug.com/`):

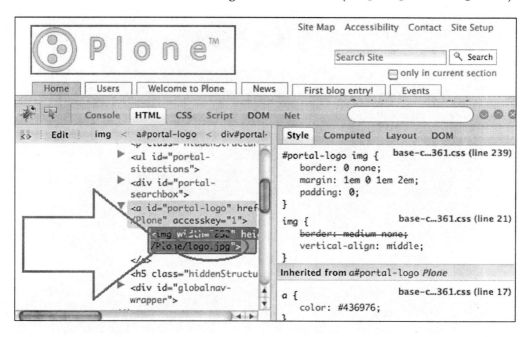

The next step is to add a file of the same name to the custom images folder in our theme package.

You can use any image, but we will use `plone-logo-128-white-bg.png` from the Plone logo pack on plone.org (`http://plone.org/foundation/logo/the-plone-logo/`).

For adding the file just mentioned:

```
$ cp ~/Desktop/plone-logo-128-white-bg.png my.theme/my/theme/skins/my_
theme_custom_images/logo.jpg
```

Now without restarting Plone (assuming you are running it in the foreground with bin/instance fg), reload the front page and you should see:

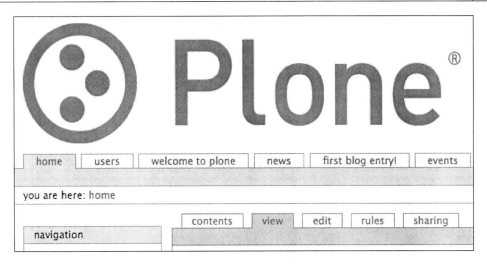

This is a simple example of customizing Plone with a filesystem theme package. We can customize many aspects of Plone's appearance using this technique.

Why did this work?

You may wonder why we copied `plone-logo-128-white-bg.png` to `logo.jpg`. The **short answer** is because it works, and the file extension does not matter.

The **medium length answer** is that we have registered a new filesystem directory view and it is higher in the skin resolution order than Plone's filesystem directory view. Both contain an object called `logo.jpg`, but ours is discovered first.

The **long answer** is that there is a feature in Zope 2 called **Acquisition** that makes this customization possible (`http://docs.zope.org/zope2/zope2book/Acquisition.html`). In addition to the (core) Acquisition feature, there is a powerful add-on called the Content Management Framework (CMF) that Plone uses extensively. Plone registers a filesystem directory view and adds resources to it; then we customize a resource by ensuring it is acquired before Plone's resource is acquired.

Examining themes in the Zope Management Interface

Now that we have seen in part how themes work, let us take a closer look at their representation in **Zope Object Database (ZODB)**.

Browse to `http://localhost:8080/Plone`. Click on **Site Setup | Zope Management Interface** and you should see:

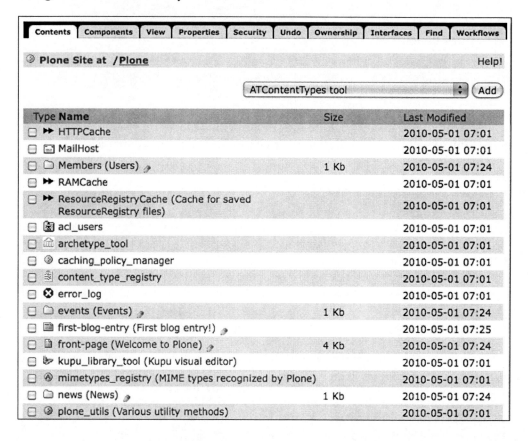

This is a **Through the Web (TTW)** representation of all the objects in the database at the Plone site level (the application root is one level above).

The most frequently used theme-related objects here are:

- `portal_css`
- `portal_javascripts`
- `portal_skins`
- `portal_view_customizations`

Of these, `portal_css` and `portal_javascripts` are most often used to enable their respective debug modes, wherein the CSS and JavaScript files are not compiled into a single file (not to be confused with Zope 2's debug mode which detects filesystem changes in real time when enabled).

Take a look at your site with Firebug, in particular the style tab.

You should see:

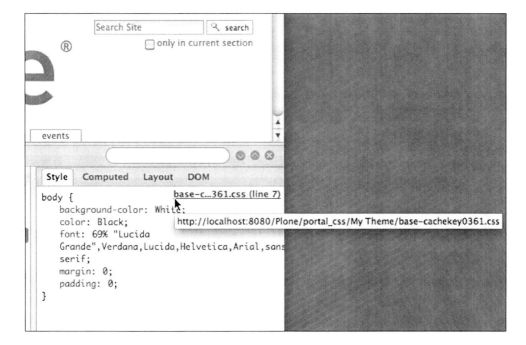

Now enable debug mode in `portal_javascripts` and look again. You should see:

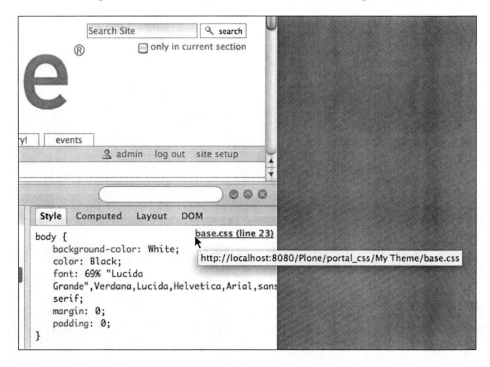

When `portal_css` debug mode is enabled, we can see (or by viewing the HTML source) that the CSS files are loaded individually in Firebug.

The same applies to `portal_javascripts` debug mode.

This can be absolutely invaluable when trying to correlate various visual elements with their respective sources.

In addition to debug mode, you can also add CSS/JavaScript files to their respective registries through the Web, which brings us to the next topic.

Making changes through the Web

Let us continue our ZMI walkthrough by examining both `portal_skins` and `portal_view_customizations`.

portal_skins

Browse to `http://localhost:8080/Plone`. Click on **Site Setup | Zope Management Interface | portal_skins**.

You should see:

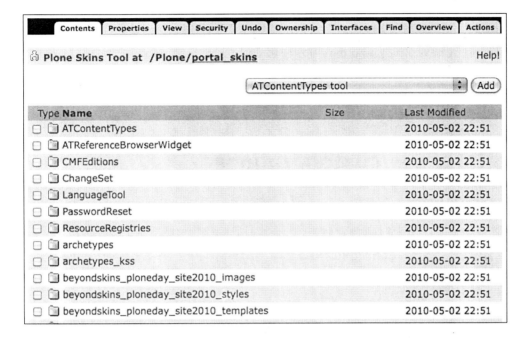

If you scroll down and click on **my_theme_custom_images** you will find the image you added earlier:

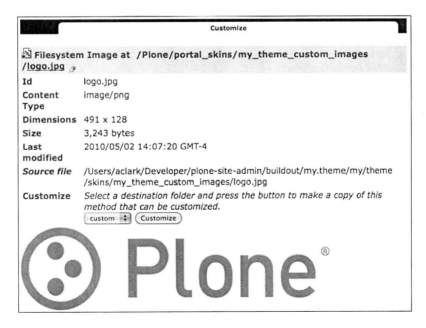

If you wanted to upload a new image, you could click the **Customize** button and upload it, but keep in mind that change will only exist in the database.

Assuming you want to keep the my.theme package up-to-date (in a software repository for example), you may prefer to customize the image on the filesystem (and resist the temptation to customize it through the Web).

If you do customize through the Web, consider the changes only temporary or volatile.

portal_view_customizations

Next up is portal_view_customizations where we will explore yet another way to customize the logo.

Browse to http://localhost:8080/Plone. Click on **Site Setup | Zope Management Interface | portal_view_customizations | zope.interface.interface | plone.logo**.

You should see:

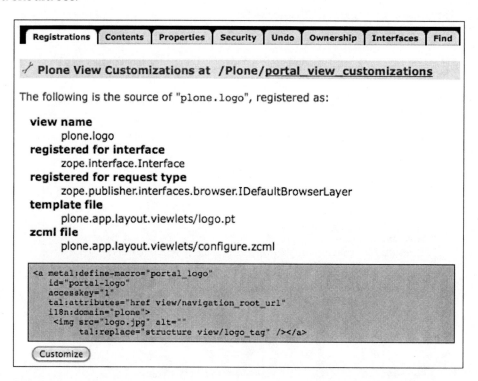

If you wanted to, you could click the **Customize** button and change the image tag code:

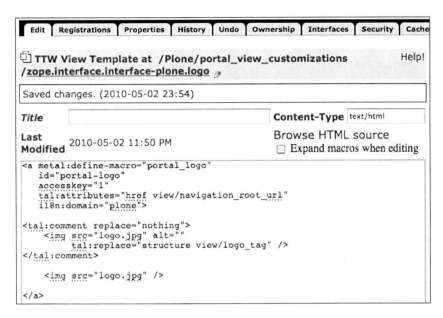

Since we used the same file (`logo.jpg`), the site will look exactly the same.

But now you can upload a new image and change the code as you see fit. To demonstrate this, let us now browse to `http://localhost:8080/Plone` and click on **Site Setup | Zope Management Interface | portal_skins | custom** and add an image:

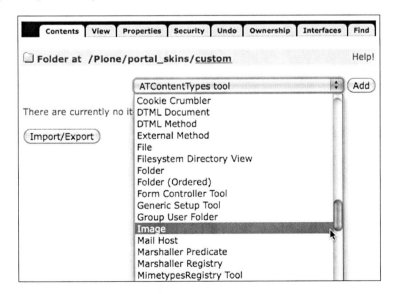

You can use any image you like, but we will use `Vlogo250.gif` from the Zope logo pack: `http://www.zope.com/about_us/legal/low_res.zip`.

Now return to `http://localhost:8080/Plone` and click on **Site Setup | Zope Management Interface | portal_view_customizations | zope.interface.interface | plone.logo** and change the filename to `Vlogo250.gif`:

```
<a metal:define-macro="portal_logo"
    id="portal-logo"
    accesskey="1"
    tal:attributes="href view/navigation_root_url"
    i18n:domain="plone">

<tal:comment replace="nothing">
    <img src="logo.jpg" alt=""
        tal:replace="structure view/logo_tag" />
</tal:comment>

    <img src="Vlogo250.gif" />

</a>
```

You should see:

Summary

That's it for this chapter. We have just demonstrated several ways to customize Plone's appearance with (hopefully) simple examples to convey the pros and cons of each method.

You have learned:

- How to browse for themes on plone.org and install them with Buildout
- How to use Omelette and Python to examine theme package contents
- About theme package contents
- How to create a theme package, and perform a simple customization
- How to find your way around the ZMI
- How to customize themes through the Web

See you in Chapter 4, where we will discuss site administration, including user and group management with LDAP.

4
Administration

If you have read any of the online Plone documentation or Plone books, you will notice that most of the topics covered in this book are not new. What is new is the Buildout-driven approach to site management. Buildout has been covered before, but only as an aside. A modern Plone site is comprised of many parts that may be tedious to assemble by hand. Fortunately, Buildout lends itself to the task.

Another tool, **Make** (`http://www.gnu.org/software/make/`), is perhaps equally well-suited to the task. If you are familiar with Make, Buildout should feel somewhat familiar. The first difference between them is the configuration file syntax. Another difference is that Make is written in C, and is typically used to compile C code, whereas Buildout is written in Python, and is typically used to assemble Python packages. Although they are different in many ways, both the tools share similar concepts:

- Building targets or parts
- Controlling the build process with configuration files
- Detecting and reacting to changes on disk

But we digress—whether you were familiar with Buildout or Make before reading this book does not matter. After reading it, you will be familiar with Buildout and will know how to use it to manage your Plone site.

At this point, we have discussed topics like installing Python, bootstrapping a Plone site, and changing the appearance.

In this chapter, we will discuss user management, group management, and related tasks.

You will learn:

- Configuring mail settings in a development environment
- Out of the box user and group management
- User and group management, with LDAP

Configuring mail settings in a development environment

We will proceed to user and group management shortly. But first, let us address an important concern—how to configure the mail settings when your site is in development.

If you browse to `http://localhost:8080/Plone` and click on **Site Setup** on your newly-created Plone site, you should see:

Warning You have not configured a mail host or a site 'From' address, various features including contact forms, email notification and password reset will not work. Go to the Mail control panel to fix this.

This warning message was designed to encourage folks to configure their mail settings now, rather than waiting for an error message to appear later, in case they failed to do so.

However, the need for the warning message mostly applies only to production sites. In development, you may not be running a mail server locally (that is, on your laptop), or you may not have access to the production mail servers, a mail server you can test with, and so on.

Having to configure the mail settings in production is expected, but having to configure them in development can be a mild annoyance. Nevertheless, having the mail server working in development is often quite handy, if not absolutely necessary.

Setting up the mail host

You could use your own mail server, assuming you have one and know the settings for setting up the mail host.

Alternatively, you can create a free Gmail account (if you do not have one already) and use Google's Gmail service (`http://gmail.com`) to configure mail settings in Plone.

To configure mail settings using a Gmail account, click on the **Mail control panel** link as suggested, or browse to `http://localhost:8080/Plone`. Then, click on **Site Settings | Mail** and enter your Gmail account settings.

You should see (something like):

SMTP server ▪
The address of your local SMTP (outgoing e-mail) server. Usually 'localhost', unless you use an external server to send e-mail.

```
smtp.gmail.com
```

SMTP port ▪
The port of your local SMTP (outgoing e-mail) server. Usually '25'.

```
25
```

ESMTP username
Username for authentication to your e-mail server. Not required unless you are using ESMTP.

```
clark.alex@gmail.com
```

ESMTP password
The password for the ESMTP user account.

```
••••••••••••
```

Also, enter your name and e-mail address in the **Site 'From' name** and **Site 'From' address** respectively, and click on **Save**.

You should now be able to use the contact form, add new users, and do anything in Plone that requires Plone to send mail.

Avoiding the mail host

If you want to avoid configuring your mail settings, but want to proceed with user and group management, you could browse to `http://localhost:8080/Plone`. Then, click on **Site Setup | Security settings**.

You should see:

☐ **Let users select their own passwords**
If not selected, passwords will be autogenerated and mailed to users, which verifies that they have entered a valid email address.

Check the box and click on **Save**.

You should now be able to create users without configuring mail settings, because Plone will not be required to send mail when it creates users.

Other tasks, such as using the contact form will still fail.

Of course, allowing users to register without verifying an e-mail address presents its own set of problems, and more importantly, it presents the potential for abuse; so be careful.

Faking the mail host

Alternatively, you can enter bogus mail settings and force Plone to send a mail to the terminal by using Martin Aspeli's **PrintingMailHost** (http://pypi.python.org/pypi/Products.PrintingMailHost).

In 04-administration-mailhost.cfg, we have:

```
[buildout]
extends = 03-appearance-zopeskel.cfg

[instance]
#eggs += Products.PrintingMailHost
```

You should now uncomment the eggs parameter to make 04-administration-mailhost.cfg look like this:

```
[buildout]
extends = 03-appearance-zopeskel.cfg

[instance]
eggs += Products.PrintingMailHost
```

Now stop Plone (with *Ctrl + C* or *Ctrl + Z/Enter*) and run Buildout:

```
$ bin/buildout -c 04-administration-mailhost.cfg
```

You should see:

```
$ bin/buildout -c 04-administration-mailhost.cfg

...

Getting distribution for 'Products.PrintingMailHost'.

Got Products.PrintingMailHost 0.7.

...
```

Now start Plone:

```
$ bin/instance fg
```

You should see:

```
$ bin/instance fg
...
Hold on to your hats folks, I'm a-patchin'
2010-05-16 14:22:03 WARNING PrintingMailHost


*************************************************************************


Monkey patching MailHosts to print emails to the terminal instead of
sending them.


NO MAIL WILL BE SENT FROM ZOPE AT ALL!


Turn off debug mode or remove PrintingMailHost from the Products
directory to turn this off.


*************************************************************************


...

2010-05-16 14:22:09 INFO Zope Ready to handle requests
```

And now, if you browse to `http://localhost:8080/Plone`, click on **Contact**, fill in the contact form, and click on **Send**, you should see:

```
---- sending mail ----
...
You are receiving this mail because Alex Clark
aclark@aclark.net
is sending feedback about the site administered by you at http://
localhost:8080/Plone.
The message sent was:


This site is great!
...
```

In other words, instead of trying to send the mail, Plone will print it.

Do not forget to disable the PrintingMailHost if you do not want this behavior.

Though the warning message suggests removing it from the products directory, we have not installed the old-style Zope 2 product package (rather, we have installed the new-style Python egg package with the help of Buildout). So, just re-comment the eggs parameter of the `instance` section, as shown:

```
[buildout]
extends = 03-appearance-zopeskel.cfg


[instance]
#eggs += Products.PrintingMailHost
```

Now stop Plone (with *Ctrl + C* or *Ctrl + Z/ Enter*) and run Buildout:

```
$ bin/buildout -c 04-administration-mailhost.cfg
```

Now start Plone:

```
$ bin/instance fg
```

This effectively configures the `04-administration-mailhost.cfg` file to do nothing, as it is configured to do so by default.

User and group management: Out of the box

For many organizations, a few users (in a few groups with a few roles) are enough to satisfy their content-publishing needs. Other organizations may have more complex needs, and may require more than the out of the box (OOB) feature set.

In this chapter, we will focus on LDAP integration to handle these needs. However, let us cover the out of the box feature set first.

The Zope 2 administrator account

The Zope 2 administrator is a user at the Zope 2 application root level that has the Manager role. You will need this user at least initially to use Plone (for example, to create a Plone site object).

Conveniently, the **plone.recipe.zope2instance** recipe (`http://pypi.python.org/pypi/plone.recipe.zope2instance`) assists us with the creation of a Zope 2 administrator.

All you have to do is to configure the `user` parameter in the `instance` section of your Buildout configuration file, and run Buildout:

```
[instance]
...
user = admin:admin
```

However, note that this user exists in the database only (ZODB). Also, keep in mind that once this user exists, subsequent Buildout runs will not affect it. In other words, you cannot change the password for an existing user by changing it in your Buildout configuration file.

Plone supports users and groups for the purpose of adding and editing content. If you are not familiar with how to manage users and groups, see Chapter 8 of *"Practical Plone 3", Packt Publishing* (`https://www.packtpub.com/practical-plone-3-beginners-guide-to-building-powerful-websites/book`).

Once you have created a Plone site with users and groups within it, the top-level Zope 2 user becomes secondary (but is still important). A good rule of thumb is to treat the top-level Zope 2 administrator like an administrator in Windows, or like a root user in Mac OS X and Ubuntu Linux (and any UNIX)—use it only when you need it.

A potential source of confusion is that the top-level Zope 2 user can log in to the Plone site, but does not exist in the Plone site. To demonstrate this, browse to `http://localhost:8080/Plone`, click on **Site Setup | Users and Groups**, and click on **Show all**.

You should see:

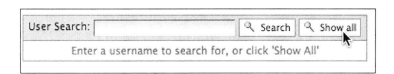

In other words, you see nothing, because Plone users do not exist yet. This is a good time to create a Plone administrator (that is, a user with the role of a Manager).

This user will be able to manage the Plone site, but not the Zope 2 application above it.

The Plone administrator account

Now that you have configured the mail settings (or either avoided configuring them or faked them) you can browse to `http://localhost:8080/Plone` and click on **Site Setup | Users and Groups** to add a user.

Once you add a user, you can configure him or her to be an administrator by following these steps:

Browse to `http://localhost:8080/Plone`, then click on **Site Setup | Users and Groups | <user> | Group memberships | Quick search**.

1. Enter **Administrators** in the text field and click on **Search**.
2. Check the box next to **Administrators** and click **Add user to selected group**.

You should be aware that we added this user to the Administrators group, rather than just assigning the role of a Manager directly to the user, which may be easier.

This method makes it easier to perform batch operations on a group of users later. Batch operations can include changing roles, sharing content, removing or disabling users, and so on.

In Plone 4

In Plone 4, groups can be nested. Visit `http://dev.plone.org/plone/ticket/5683` for more information.

Also, in Plone 4, you can add users to groups immediately using the add user form. Visit `http://dev.plone.org/plone/ticket/9330` for more information.

You should see:

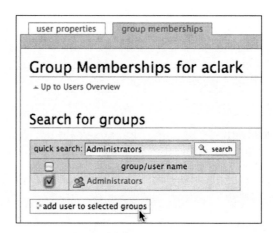

You are now free to add additional users and groups with this account, as well as to perform other administrative tasks that require the Manager role. Now, you are also free to log out of the top-level Zope 2 account until you need it again, which will probably be infrequent. In fact, it may be so infrequent that you may forget the password—no problem!

Resetting the password

We learned in Chapter 2 how to change the admin user's password through the Web, but what happens if you forget the password?

You can use the `bin/instance` script to create a new administrator, like this:

```
$ bin/instance adduser admin2 some-password
```

But if the admin user exists already, do not try to reset the password, like this:

```
$ bin/instance adduser admin some-password
```

This command will fail silently, and you will wonder why it did not work. To avoid this problem, create another user first, for example admin2, and then log in with admin2 to reset admin user's password; remove the admin2 user if you like after that.

Users and groups management with LDAP

One of the downsides of adding users and groups in this way is that they only exist in the Plone database (ZODB) and as such, may be difficult to manage in large numbers.

Not to mention, you may need to deploy to an organization where an existing user database is in use (for example, LDAP or **Active Directory** (**AD**).

Connecting Plone to LDAP and Active Directory is covered in detail in Chapter 21 of "*Practical Plone 3*", *Packt Publishing* (`https://www.packtpub.com/practical-plone-3-beginners-guide-to-building-powerful-websites/book`). So, we will not repeat all of that information here (although there is some overlap).

We will not cover the installation of OpenLDAP or Active Directory, too. We will assume you (or a system administrator) can manage the task (if it is required by your organization).

What we will cover here is the installation and setup of `plone.app.ldap`, with a particular focus on how Buildout works, and how to achieve results as quickly as possible in Plone (as well as how to avoid pitfalls).

Installing OpenLDAP

If you need help installing OpenLDAP, there is a particularly good tutorial available here: `http://www.debian-administration.org/article/OpenLDAP_installation_on_Debian`.

While the installation is Debian-specific, most of everything else is not. In other words, if you are able to install OpenLDAP, you can follow the tutorial to perform the rest of the configuration steps.

Adding plone.app.ldap to the Buildout

In `04-administration-ldap.cfg`, we have:

```
[buildout]
extends = 03-appearance-zopeskel.cfg

[instance]
eggs += plone.app.ldap
zcml += plone.app.ldap
```

We have extended the last known good configuration and have added `plone.app.ldap` to the `eggs` and `zcml` parameters in the `instance` section. The current list of eggs now looks like this:

```
eggs = Plone
    collective.portlet.sitemap
    collective.portlet.explore
    webcouturier.dropdownmenu
    Products.Scrawl
    beyondskins.ploneday.site2010
    plone.app.ldap
```

You can get this information by running Buildout, then looking at the `installed.cfg` file in the root directory of your buildout.

Now stop Plone (with *Ctrl* + *C* or *Ctrl* + *Z/Enter*) and run Buildout:

```
$ bin/buildout -c 04-administration-ldap.cfg
```

You should see:

```
...

Installing instance.
Getting distribution for 'plone.app.ldap'.
Got plone.app.ldap 1.2.1.
Getting distribution for 'Products.PloneLDAP'.
Got Products.PloneLDAP 1.1.
Getting distribution for 'Products.LDAPUserFolder'.
...

Got Products.LDAPUserFolder 2.16.
Getting distribution for 'Products.LDAPMultiPlugins'.
Got Products.LDAPMultiPlugins 1.9.
Getting distribution for 'dataflake.ldapconnection'.
Got dataflake.ldapconnection 1.0.
Getting distribution for 'python-ldap>=2.0.6'.
extra_compile_args:
extra_objects:
...

Got python-ldap 2.3.11.
Getting distribution for 'dataflake.cache'.
Got dataflake.cache 1.1.
...
```

You will notice that `plone.app.ldap` and its dependencies are now installed.

Python-LDAP package dependencies

You should experience trouble-free installations of `plone.app.ldap` (and its dependencies such as python-ldap) on fresh installs of Mac OS X and Ubuntu Linux with the following two exceptions:

On Ubuntu Linux you must install the `libsasl2-dev` and `libldap2-dev` packages (and optionally the `libssl-dev` package).

On Windows, it is necessary to install the **python-ldap** package via the binary installer (for Python 2.4), available from the Python Package Index (`http://pypi.python.org/packages/2.4/p/python-ldap/python-ldap-2.3.11.win32-py2.4.exe`).

Now start Plone:

```
$ bin/instance fg
```

Adding plone.app.ldap to Plone

If you browse to `http://localhost:8080/Plone` and then click on **Site Setup |
Add-on Products**, you should see:

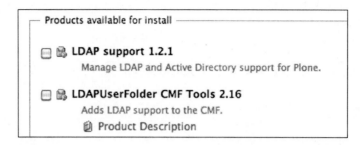

Two LDAP-related packages are now listed as **available for install**, only
one of which is actually installable. If you click on the product description of
`LDAPUserFolder`, you will see this message:

> *NOTE: Do not install the CMFLDAP GenericSetup extension profile into a Plone
> site. They are meant for pure CMF sites only and will break Plone.*

In other words, do not install LDAPUserFolder in Plone. Instead, install only the
LDAP support package.

Do not install LDAPUserFolder in Plone

Why not? The **short answer** is that even though the package appears
in **Add-on products**, it is not compatible with Plone.

The **medium length answer** is that as the documentation in the
product description states that LDAPUserFolder is compatible with
pure CMF sites. This means that replacing the top-level Pluggable
Auth Service (`http://pypi.python.org/pypi/Products.
PluggableAuthService`) object (`/acl_users` at the Plone site
level) would break Plone.

The **long answer** is that Plone uses an add-on for Zope 2 called the
Pluggable Auth Service to facilitate users and groups management
(among other things). When you install plone.app.ldap, it will install
PloneLDAP (`http://pypi.python.org/pypi/Products.
PloneLDAP`), which will install the other dependencies (for
example, LDAPMultiPlugins and LDAPUserFolder) and create
an LDAPUserFolder for you inside the LDAP plugin, inside the
Pluggable Auth Service (Plone level acl_users object).

Next, browse to `http://localhost:8080/Plone`, click on **Site Setup | Add-on
Product Configuration | LDAP Connection | LDAP Servers**, and add a server.

To verify the connection, browse to `http://localhost:8080/Plone` and click on
**Site Setup | Zope Management Interface | acl_users | ldap-plugin | Contents |
acl_users | LDAP Servers**.

You should see:

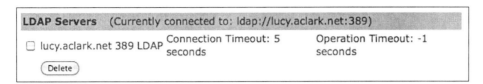

Configuring plone.app.ldap

We now have five more tasks to perform, all of which can be done simultaneously (or
separately, if you like) in the **Global Settings** tab of the **LDAP configuration** form:

- Configure the RDN, user id, and login name attributes
- Configure the bind DN and password
- Configure the LDAP object classes
- Configure the base DN for users and groups
- Restart Plone (to force re-connect the LDAP connection)

However, before we begin those tasks, let us take a minute to define the terminology
we are using.

LDAP Terminology

What follows here is a very brief overview of LDAP terminology. See Chapter 21
of *"Practical Plone 3"*, *Packt Publishing* (`https://www.packtpub.com/practical-
plone-3-beginners-guide-to-building-powerful-websites/book`) for
more details.

DN

To understand the **LDAP configuration** form and **Global Settings** in particular, you
need to understand (if you do not already) that one of the core features of LDAP is to
provide a way to organize hierarchical data using unique string identifiers such as:

`dn: uid=aclark,ou=People,dc=aclark,dc=net`

The entry above is a **Distinguished Name** (**DN**), or a uniquely identifiable entry. We
are simplifying this explanation of course, for brevity's sake. For more information,
visit `http://www.zytrax.com/books/ldap/`.

DC, UID, OU

In case these terms are not obvious, they are acronyms for **Domain Component (DC)** **User ID (UID)**, and **Organizational Unit (OU)** respectively.

RDN

Distinguished names are comprised of **Relative Distinguished Names (RDNs)**.

A common way to explain them is to compare them with Internet hostnames, which have a corresponding fully-qualified domain name.

For example, in the case of the host `lucy.aclark.net`, `lucy` and `aclark.net` are both relative distinguished names, while `lucy.aclark.net` is a distinguished name, that is it is unique within the hierarchal data.

Bind DN and password

In order to use LDAP in Plone, you must provide Plone with a DN and an associated password which it can use to authenticate with the LDAP server defined in the **LDAP Servers** section of the **LDAP configuration** form.

Attributes and object classes

Object classes are collections of attributes, and attributes are containers of data (again, we are simplifying for brevity's sake).

Entering the form data

With the information above, we know enough to fill in the **Global Settings** of the **LDAP configuration** form.

LDAP server type

We assume the server type to be OpenLDAP because it is the most robust implementation. An Active Directory implementation will support only "read-only access".

RDN attribute

Here, we are asked which of the following LDAP attributes we would like to use as a part of the LDAP DN used to create new users: CN, Mail, SN, or UID. While the default choice is CN, the most common choice is UID, which will create a DN like this:

```
dn: uid=aclark,ou=People,dc=aclark,dc=net
```

User id attribute

Here, we are asked which of the following LDAP attributes we would like Plone to use internally to identify users: CN, Mail, SN, or UID. While the default choice is CN, the most common choice is UID.

Login name attribute

Here, we are asked which of the following LDAP attributes we would like to use for the Plone user account login name: CN, Mail, SN, or UID. In other words, it asks for the name the user types into the login form. While the default choice is CN, the most common choice is UID.

LDAP object classes

Setting the object class tells LDAP where to look for your objects. If you were to follow the LDAP tutorial on `http://www.debian-administration.org/article/ OpenLDAP_installation_on_Debian`, you would notice that new users are created with the person object class: `http://www.debian-administration.org/article/ OpenLDAP_installation_on_Debian#id2503051`.

In the case of our example, the `aclark` user looks like this:

```
# aclark, People, aclark.net
dn: uid=aclark,ou=People,dc=aclark,dc=net
uid: aclark
uidNumber: 20000
gidNumber: 20000
objectClass: top
objectClass: person
objectClass: posixAccount
objectClass: shadowAccount
loginShell: /bin/bash
homeDirectory: /home/aclark
sn: Alex Clark
cn: Alex Clark
```

This means we must configure the `person` object class in the **LDAP object classes** field in **Global Settings**.

Bind DN and password

As mentioned earlier, we must configure an LDAP admin user in Plone to allow Plone to connect to our LDAP server as an administrator.

In the `aclark` example, the LDAP admin user looks like this:

```
# admin, aclark.net
dn: cn=admin,dc=aclark,dc=net
objectClass: simpleSecurityObject
objectClass: organizationalRole
cn: admin
description: LDAP administrator
```

This means we must configure the `cn=admin,dc=aclark,dc=net`, and bind DN in the **Bind DN** field in **Global Settings**.

Also, as mentioned earlier, this LDAP account has an associated password. If you are not familiar with how to install and configure OpenLDAP, create an admin account, and set the password. You can refer to `http://www.debian-administration.org/article/OpenLDAP_installation_on_Debian#ldap-install`.

If you are not using Debian (one of our target operating systems, Ubuntu Linux, is based on Debian at least) and have installed OpenLDAP from source (or vendor package), you can visit `http://www.openldap.org/doc/admin24/quickstart.html`.

In other words, you should be able to specify the LDAP admin user's password in the **Bind password** field in **Global Settings**.

Base DN and search scope for users and groups

Following the `aclark` example, the base-distinguished names for users and groups are as follows:

```
# People, aclark.net
dn: ou=People,dc=aclark,dc=net
ou: People
objectClass: organizationalUnit

# Group, aclark.net
dn: ou=Group,dc=aclark,dc=net
ou: Group
objectClass: organizationalUnit
```

This means that we will configure the `ou=People,dc=aclark,dc=net` and `ou=Group,dc=aclark,dc=net` base-distinguished names for users and groups, respectively.

We will leave the default settings for scope, since we are not particularly concerned with whether or not the sub-objects are searched. If you like, you can try the one-level setting, which should work equally well in this case.

Restarting Plone

At this point, it may be necessary to restart Plone in order to force a reconnection with the LDAP server.

Alternatively, you could browse to `http://localhost:8080/Plone` and click on **Site Setup | Add-on Product Configuration | LDAP Connection | LDAP Servers**.

You should see:

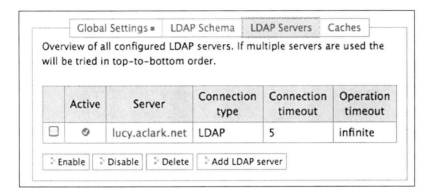

Check the box next to the server, and click on **Disable**. Then check the box next to the server and click on **Enable**.

Using LDAP in Plone

At this point, you should be able to see LDAP users in Plone.

If you browse to `http://localhost:8080/Plone` and click on **Site Setup | Users and Groups | Show all**, you should be able to see your LDAP users (or `aclark` in the case of our example):

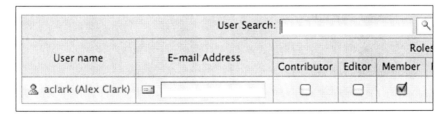

This user can log in to Plone as a member (user with Member role).

To configure LDAP users to be administrators, you could add them to the (ZODB-only) Administrators group in Plone (like we did earlier in this chapter).

Alternatively, you could create a group in LDAP, assign it the Manager role, and add users to that group.

Creating and using LDAP groups

The most straightforward way to do this is to browse to `http://localhost:8080/Plone`, click on **Site Setup | Zope Management Interface | acl_users | ldap-plugin | Contents | acl_users | Groups**.

You should see:

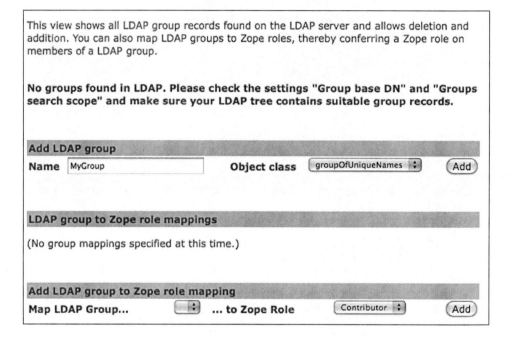

Here, you can add a group, for example **MyGroup,** and map it to the **Manager** role. You should see the following:

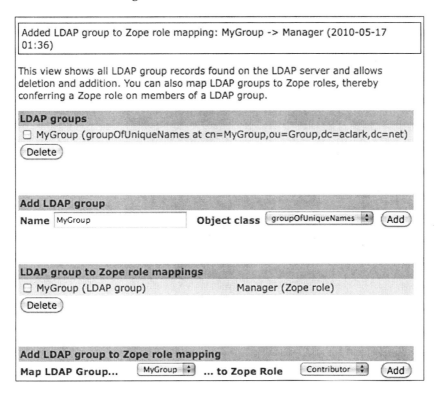

Restarting Plone

Again at this point, it may be necessary to restart Plone in order to force a reconnection with the LDAP server.

Adding users to MyGroup

After you restart Plone, you should be able to add users to the (LDAP-only) **MyGroup** group in Plone (like we did earlier in this chapter).

Since we mapped **MyGroup** to the Manager role, anyone in this group will be able to perform administrative tasks.

Summary

That is all for this chapter. Nice job following along!

You have learned:

- How to configure mail settings in a development environment
- How to configure users and groups with the out of the box feature set
- How to configure users and groups with LDAP

Join me again in Chapter 5, where we will discuss maintenance topics such as database packing and how to back up your database. More importantly, we will discuss how to automate these tasks in production.

5
Deployment and Maintenance

This chapter marks a significant turning point for us in this book. Up until now, we have only discussed development issues (more or less). For the next four chapters, we will only discuss deployment/maintenance issues (more or less).

Do you remember the site administration diagram, located at the beginning of Chapter 1? A fair amount of development tasks have now been covered, so we can now switch to deployment/maintenance tasks with confidence, knowing that we understand what the various development tasks look like. Also, remember that in the real world, you are likely to have deployed to staging numerous times before deploying to production.

In a way, you have already been prepared for what is coming next. By demonstrating Buildout's ability to extend configuration files, we have (hopefully) shown that a production buildout is just a buildout configuration file(s) that configures the site for production use.

In some cases, a production buildout may get so elaborate that it works only in production. In the other cases, it may work just fine in both development and production environments. For example, a production buildout may configure packages to depend on libraries whose locations vary, depending on the environment. Hence, a production buildout may not work in development because the libraries are in a different place.

At this point, it may become more desirable to include such dependencies in the buildout, but that is for you to decide. There is always a trade-off while deciding what dependencies to include in the buildout, versus what (operating system vendor packages) dependencies to rely on in production. A good rule of thumb is to install as many vendor packages as possible, and then use Buildout to install the rest.

In our first example, we will demonstrate what a typical production configuration file looks like. Then, we will demonstrate the techniques to automate various maintenance tasks. Lastly, we will discuss the remaining miscellaneous tasks, if any, which relate to deployment and maintenance.

In this chapter, you will learn the following:

- Creating a production buildout
- Backing up your database
- Automating database backups
- Restoring your database from a backup
- Packing your database
- Automating database packing
- Rotating logs

Creating a production buildout

We would be remiss at this point if we did not discuss adding **Zope Enterprise Objects (ZEOs)** to our buildout. ZEO provides a way to allow numerous Zope 2 instances to access the same database (Data.fs file).

During a normal operation (that is, without ZEO), Zope 2 locks the Data.fs file when it is in use. When ZEO is in use, it locks the file too, but allows connections over TCP/IP.

So from now on, we will be using ZEO. This will enable us to do a number of things:

- Learn how to use ZEO
- Establish additional connections to the database to facilitate
    - Backups
    - Debugging
    - Database packing
    - Load balancing

However, if we were to add ZEO to our current buildout, we would experience this problem:

```
$ bin/buildout -c 05-deployment-maintenance-production.cfg
Updating zope2.
Updating fake eggs
```

```
Updating instance.

Installing plonesite.

2010-05-19 22:27:32 WARNING ZEO.zrpc (10025) CW: error connecting to
('127.0.0.1', 8100): ECONNREFUSED
```

This is because in 05-deployment-maintenance-production.cfg, we reconfigure the instance section to use ZEO, but we do not have a ZEO installed yet (because the add ZEO buildout run has not yet been completed).

At the same time, the plonesite part is trying to start the instance so that it can create a Plone site. However, the Zope 2 instance is unable to connect to a ZEO instance since it is not running and does not exist yet (unless the add ZEO buildout run completes).

To work around this, we can create a configuration file to subtract the plonesite part from the list of parts:

```
[buildout]
extends = 04-administration-ldap.cfg
parts -= plonesite
```

Note that we are using the -= notation for the first time.

Until now, we have only been adding parts to the parts parameter. In this case, we are subtracting the plonesite part to make the add ZEO buildout run work properly.

If we need the plonesite part later, we can easily add it back.

Next, we configure ZEO in 05-deployment-maintenance-production.cfg by adding adding a zeo section, and by configuring the instance section to be a ZEO client:

```
[buildout]
extends = 05-deployment-maintenance-plonesite.cfg
parts += zeo

[instance]
zeo-client = True

[zeo]
recipe = plone.recipe.zope2zeoserver
zope2-location = ${zope2:location}
```

Now run Buildout:

```
$ bin/buildout -c 05-deployment-maintenance-production.cfg
```

You should see:

```
$ bin/buildout -c 05-deployment-maintenance-production.cfg
Getting distribution for 'plone.recipe.zope2zeoserver==1.4'.
Got plone.recipe.zope2zeoserver 1.4.

...

Installing zeo.
Created directory /Users/aclark/Developer/plone-site-admin/buildout/
parts/zeo
Created directory /Users/aclark/Developer/plone-site-admin/buildout/
parts/zeo/etc
Created directory /Users/aclark/Developer/plone-site-admin/buildout/
parts/zeo/var
Created directory /Users/aclark/Developer/plone-site-admin/buildout/
parts/zeo/log
Created directory /Users/aclark/Developer/plone-site-admin/buildout/
parts/zeo/bin
Wrote file /Users/aclark/Developer/plone-site-admin/buildout/parts/zeo/
etc/zeo.conf
Wrote file /Users/aclark/Developer/plone-site-admin/buildout/parts/zeo/
bin/zeoctl
Changed mode for /Users/aclark/Developer/plone-site-admin/buildout/parts/
zeo/bin/zeoctl to 755
Wrote file /Users/aclark/Developer/plone-site-admin/buildout/parts/zeo/
bin/runzeo
Changed mode for /Users/aclark/Developer/plone-site-admin/buildout/parts/
zeo/bin/runzeo to 755
Generated script '/Users/aclark/Developer/plone-site-admin/buildout/bin/
zeo'.
Generated script '/Users/aclark/Developer/plone-site-admin/buildout/bin/
zeopack'.
```

Now start ZEO:

```
$ bin/zeo start
. daemon process started, pid=10578
```

Now start Plone:

```
$ bin/instance fg
```

Now, we can move on to backups.

Backing up your database

Database backups are an important part of any web application deployment, and Plone is no exception.

However, unlike a lot of web applications, there is no SQL data to backup. This is because Plone uses Zope 2, which uses the ZODB (`http://pypi.python.org/pypi/ZODB3`) for persistent storage. The ZODB is an object database (not a relational database) and its contents are typically stored in a single flat file called `Data.fs`.

By using the undo feature of Zope 2, you can often avert disasters by undoing a transaction or more from the **Undo** form, but you must do so sequentially starting from the most recent transaction.

If you want to examine the **Undo** form, browse to `http://localhost:8080/Plone` and click on **Site Setup | Zope Management Interface**.

You should see the **Undo** form in the list of tabs at the top, toward the right side, as shown in the following screenshot:

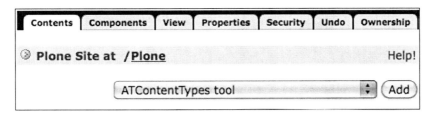

In other words, you cannot pick an arbitrary transaction from the middle of the transaction log and expect to be able to roll back to that point, without selecting all of the transactions in between.

Even if you do, it may not work. The undo feature is unfortunately not impervious to transaction conflict errors, and sometimes, we have to restore from a backup to put things right.

This is where automated "hot" backups come in handy.

The repozo utility

Copying the `Data.fs` file from one host to another off-site may suffice as a "hot" backup, but in theory you should never copy data from a running instance because you could miss data being written to the file at the time of the copy.

Lucky for us, Zope 2 ships with the `repozo` utility as a part of the ZODB3 package (`http://pypi.python.org/pypi/ZODB3`) to facilitate "hot" backups and you can use it to backup your site as shown:

```
% bin/repozo -v -B -F -f var/filestorage/Data.fs -r var/filestorage
```

The output for this should be something like this:

```
looking for files between last full backup and 2009-07-04-06-08-12...
no files found
doing a full backup
writing full backup: 4100111 bytes to var/
filestorage/2009-07-04-06-08-12.fs
```

In the example above, we forced a full backup with the `-F` flag. If you just want to run incremental backups, you can do this:

```
% bin/repozo -v -B -f var/filestorage/Data.fs -r var/filestorage
```

This command tells repozo to run in verbose mode with `-v`, create a backup with `-B`, backup the specified file with `-f`, and put the results in the directory specified by `-r`.

Making repozo easier with collective.recipe.backup

It is likely you will not want to memorize all of these commands; so, let us make the task easier by adding **collective.recipe.backup** (`http://pypi.python.org/pypi/collective.recipe.backup`) to our buildout.

By doing this, we are configuring additional scripts to be added to the `bin` directory of the buildout. These are for us to execute (or automate) at our earliest convenience.

When executed, these scripts will run `repozo` with a sensible set of defaults.

In `05-deployment-maintenance-backup.cfg`, we have:

```
[buildout]
extends = 05-deployment-maintenance-production.cfg
parts += backup

[backup]
recipe = collective.recipe.backup
```

Now run Buildout:

```
$ bin/buildout -c 05-deployment-maintenance-backup.cfg
```

You should see:

```
$ bin/buildout -c 05-deployment-maintenance-backup.cfg
Getting distribution for 'collective.recipe.backup'.
Got collective.recipe.backup 1.3.
...
Installing backup.
backup: Created /Users/aclark/Developer/plone-site-admin/buildout/var/
backups
backup: Created /Users/aclark/Developer/plone-site-admin/buildout/var/
snapshotbackups
Generated script '/Users/aclark/Developer/plone-site-admin/buildout/bin/
backup'.
Generated script '/Users/aclark/Developer/plone-site-admin/buildout/bin/
snapshotbackup'.
Generated script '/Users/aclark/Developer/plone-site-admin/buildout/bin/
restore'.
Generated script '/Users/aclark/Developer/plone-site-admin/buildout/bin/
snapshotrestore'.
```

We now have two new directories and three new scripts in our buildout. The directories we created are:

- `var/backups`
- `var/snapshotbackups`

The scripts we created are:

- `bin/backup`
- `bin/snapshotbackup`
- `bin/restore`

Thanks to collective.recipe.backup we can now run `repozo` easily, and we have a special place to put the results.

If you want to do a regular backup of your site, just run:

```
$ bin/backup
```

The backup will be stored in `var/backups`.

Every subsequent running of `bin/backup`, assuming site content has changed, will automatically create an incremental backup ending in `.deltafs`.

If you want to set aside a full backup for some other purpose, like copying to a local development environment, you can run:

```
$ bin/snapshotbackup
```

Now, copy the file from `var/snapshotbackups`.

A simple backup strategy

A full backup will be created in `var/snapshotbackups`. At this point, you may be noticing that the business of backups can be somewhat complicated. In order to be successful over time (or in other words, to have the best chance of recovering important lost data), you will need a sane backup strategy.

A very simple backup strategy is listed here:

- Daily incremental backups
- Monthly full backups
- Yearly retention

This means we must configure our incremental backups to run daily and full backups to run once a month. We will keep a directory full of backups for a period of one year and then, we will archive that directory and start over.

In the section that follows, we will cover how to implement a portion of daily incremental backups.

Automating database backups

Of course, no one wants to perform manual backups on a regular basis.

On Mac OS X and Ubuntu Linux, we can use Buildout to configure a `cron` entry for us. On Windows, since there is no `cron`, we can use the Task manager (outside our Buildout) instead.

Using z3c.recipe.usercrontab on Mac OS X and Ubuntu Linux

To configure `cron` entries with Buildout, you can use **z3c.re.backup** (`http://pypi.python.org/pypi/collective.rec.recipe.usercrontab`).

In `05-deployment-maintenance-cron.cfg`, we have:

```
[buildout]
extends = 05-deployment-maintenance-backup.cfg
parts += cron

[cron]
recipe = z3c.recipe.usercrontab
command = ${buildout:directory}/bin/backup
times = 0 0 * * *
```

We have added a `cron` section, defined `recipe` and `command` we want to run, and the number of `times` we want to run it. If you are not familiar with the `cron` syntax, refer to the following:

Field	Allowed values
Minute	0-59
Hour	0-23
Day of the month	1-31
Month	1-12 (or names, see below)
Day of the week	0-7 (0 or 7 is Sun, or use names)

A field may be an asterisk (*), which always stands for "first-last"....

Names can also be used for the Month and Day of the week fields. Use the first three letters of the particular day or month (case does not matter). Ranges or lists of names are not allowed.

This information is from the output of the command (run on Mac OS X and Linux):

```
$ man 5 crontab
```

So, the fields are listed in order, in the `times` parameter. We have created a `cron` entry that will run our `command` at the zeroth minute of the zeroth hour, every day of the month, every month, and every day of the week.

Now run Buildout:

```
$ bin/buildout -c 05-deployment-maintenance-cron.cfg
```

You should see:

```
$ bin/buildout -c 05-deployment-maintenance-cron.cfg
...
Installing cron.
```

You can check to make sure your `crontab` entry has been created by running with the help of the following command:

```
$ crontab -l
```

You should see:

```
$ crontab -l

# Generated by /Users/aclark/Developer/plone-site-admin/buildout [cron]
0 0 * * *       /Users/aclark/Developer/plone-site-admin/buildout/bin/backup
# END /Users/aclark/Developer/plone-site-admin/buildout [cron]
```

Using Task Scheduler on Windows

To schedule tasks on Windows, select **Start | All Programs | Accessories | System Tools | Task Scheduler**.

1. When the task scheduler appears, select **Create Basic Task**:

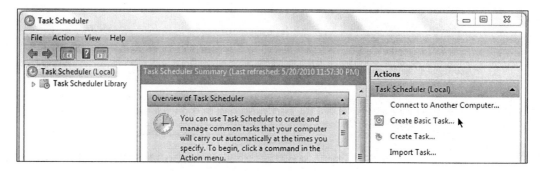

2. Next, fill in the **Name** and **Description**:

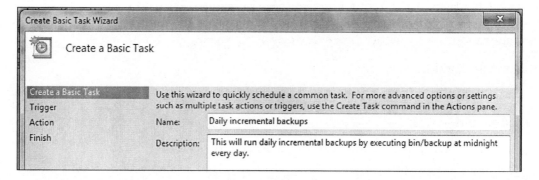

3. This is followed by when you want the task to start:

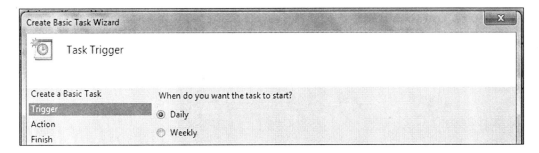

4. This is followed by when you want the task to recur:

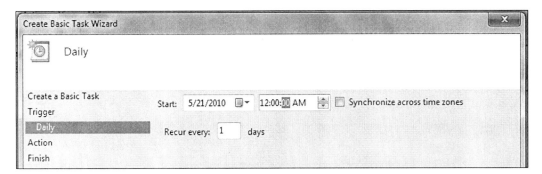

5. Next is what you want the task to do:

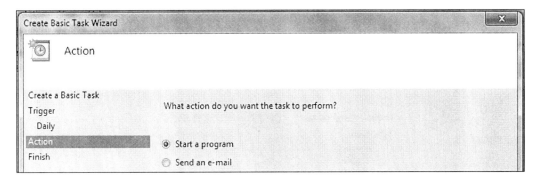

6. Select the program you want to start (for example, `C:\Users\Administrator\Developer\plone-site-admin\buildout\bin\backup.exe`). You should see:

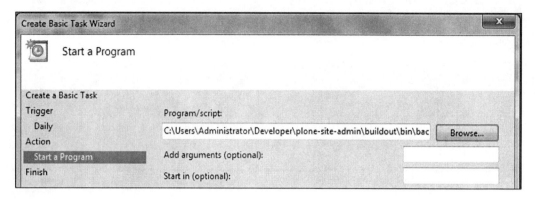

7. Click on **Finish**.

You can now test your installation by scrolling down to **Active Tasks** in the center pane, and scrolling down to your task.

You should see:

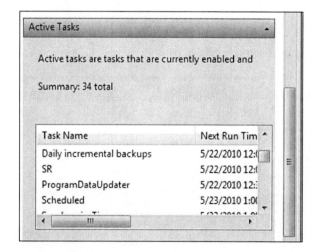

Restoring your database from a backup

If you want to restore your database from the latest backup, you can stop your site (including ZEO) and run:

```
$ bin/restore
```

In the event that you would like to know more about the process, or you would like to restore from a date prior to the last backup, you can always use the `repozo` command.

Assuming you have the backups, you can restore the data from any date by using the `-D` option:

```
% bin/repozo -R -D 2009-10-26-00-06-33 -r var/backups -o var/filestorage/
Data.fs
```

You must give `-D` a date string that matches one of your backups. It can be an incremental backup (that is, a file ending in `.deltafs`); `repozo` will figure out what to do with it.

Packing your database

Next, we will apply the same basic techniques to another important task—packing your site's database.

In Zope 2, every database transaction is saved. So if you never pack, your database will keep growing and fill up your disk. This is why we must pack; of course, how often you pack will depend on how often your site's content changes.

The recommended strategy is to pack to within seven days of the current date. In other words, keep a week's worth of transactions in the database so that you can restore to as far back as one week, if needed (assuming you are able to use undo successfully).

After you run the `05-deployment-maintenance-production.cfg` buildout, you should have a `bin/zeopack` script.

The default value is to pack to one day. If you want to change that (or the not very commonly used ZEO user/password), you can use the following parameters in the `zeo` section (which uses the **plone.recipe.zope2zeoserver** recipe):

- `pack-days`: Specifies the number of days for the `zeopack` script to retain the history. Default value is one day.
- `pack-user`: If the ZEO server uses authentication, this is the username used by the `zeopack` script to connect to the ZEO server.
- `pack-password`: If the ZEO server uses authentication, this is the password used by the `zeopack` script to connect to the ZEO server.

In the section that follows, we will cover how to implement the next portion of our simple backup policy—monthly full backups.

Automate database packing

Packing the database every month will cause the next daily backup to be a full backup instead of an incremental backup. That is because `repozo` detects the database change, and performs a full backup as a result.

This is good news for us, because it means that all we have to do to ensure monthly full backups is to configure an automated task to pack the database. In other words, we just require a `cron` entry in Mac OS X and Ubuntu Linux, and a scheduled task in Windows Task Scheduler.

We will leave the task scheduling to the Windows folks, who can easily create another scheduled task by referring to the steps we performed earlier.

For the Mac OS X and Ubuntu Linux folks, in `05-deployment-maintenance-cron2.cfg` we have the following:

```
[buildout]
extends = 05-deployment-maintenance-cron.cfg
parts += cron2

[cron2]
recipe = z3c.recipe.usercrontab
command = ${buildout:directory}/bin/zeopack
times = 0 0 1 * *
```

Notice that we chose a value of `0 0 1 * *` for the `times` parameter, to indicate that we want to perform the task on the first day of the month, at the zeroth hour, and zeroth minute.

Rotating logs

As you are probably aware, Zope 2 generates log files. Hence, we need to think about what to do when these log files grow.

Using iw.rotatezlogs on Mac OS X, Ubuntu Linux, and Windows

One of the tasks that could be difficult to standardize across operating systems is rotating Zope 2 log files. Luckily for us, there is **iw.rotatezlogs** (`http://pypi.python.org/pypi/iw.rotatezlogs`).

Although technically not a recipe, iw.rotatezlogs makes it simple to set up log rotation.

The process involves three steps:

1. Add the iw.rotatezlogs egg to the `eggs` parameter in `instance` section.
2. Add an `event-log-custom` parameter to your `instance` section with iw.rotatezlogs settings.
3. Add an `access-log-custom` parameter to your `instance` section with iw.rotatezlogs settings.

In `05-deployment-maintenance-rotate.cfg`, we have the following:

```
[buildout]
extends = 05-deployment-maintenance-cron2.cfg

[instance]
eggs += iw.rotatezlogs
event-log-custom =
    %import iw.rotatezlogs
    <rotatelogfile>
        path ${buildout:directory}/var/log/instance.log
        max-bytes 1MB
        backup-count 5
    </rotatelogfile>
access-log-custom =
    %import iw.rotatezlogs
    <rotatelogfile>
        path ${buildout:directory}/var/log/instance-Z2.log
        max-bytes 1MB
        backup-count 5
    </rotatelogfile>
```

Now run Buildout:

```
$ bin/buildout -c 05-deployment-maintenance-rotate.cfg
```

The following code should be included in `parts/instance/etc/zope.conf`:

```
...
%import iw.rotatezlogs
<rotatelogfile>
path /Users/aclark/Developer/plone-site-admin/var/log/instance.log
max-bytes 1MB
backup-count 5
</rotatelogfile>
</eventlog>
```

```
<logger access>
  level WARN

%import iw.rotatezlogs
<rotatelogfile>
path /Users/aclark/Developer/plone-site-admin/var/log/instance-Z2.log
max-bytes 1MB
backup-count 5
</rotatelogfile>
</logger>
...
```

You will notice that we have set `max-bytes` to `1MB` and `backup-count` to `5`, which means that whenever either log file reaches 1 MB, it will be rotated and when five log files are reached, the oldest one will be deleted each time a rotation occurs.

To verify this, try filling up the log files to just under 1 MB, then restart Plone. You should see the rotation occur.

Similarly, you could create five log files first, then restart Plone and you should see the rotation occur.

We can use this technique for any log files, for example ZEO.

In `05-deployment-maintenance-rotate.cfg` we have:

```
[buildout]
extends = 05-deployment-maintenance-rotate.cfg

[zeo]
eggs += iw.rotatezlogs
zeo-log-custom =
    %import iw.rotatezlogs
    <rotatelogfile>
        path ${buildout:directory}/var/log/zeo.log
        max-bytes 1MB
        backup-count 5
    </rotatelogfile>
```

Since the ZEO instance runs under its own process, you will notice that we have added the iw.rotatezlogs egg to the `zeo` section's `eggs` parameter.

At this point, we have done just about all of the setup and preparation we can do to make our site run smoothly.

Summary

In this chapter, you have learned the following:

- Adding ZEO to create a production buildout
- Using collective.recipe.backup to make using `repozo` easier
- Automating database backups with z3c.recipe.usercrontab and Task Scheduler
- Restoring your database from a backup with the help of collective. recipe.backup
- Packing your database with `zeopack`
- Automating database packing with help from z3c.recipe.usercrontab and Task Scheduler
- Rotating logs with iw.rotatezlogs

Next, in Chapter 6, we will to focus on what we can do while our site is running to monitor and optimize the performance.

Later in Chapter 7, we will cover troubleshooting and upgrading along with various security concerns.

6
Optimization

If you have made it this far, you should understand how to use Buildout to deploy your site to production by executing specific, production-ready configuration files.

We will not cover any version control systems in this book (for example, RCS, CVS, Subversion, Bazaar, Mercurial, Git), but a brief mention of version control systems in the context of our development and deployment efforts is now in order.

Throughout this book, we have been working with various Buildout configuration files. As a result, you may want to consider the following technique to manage them properly:

1. Check in buildout's configuration files to Subversion (or a version control system of your choice) when you begin your next project.
2. Check out the buildout's configuration files to the development environment.
3. Develop the buildout and commit the results.
4. Check out the buildout's configuration files to the staging and/or production server.

In the future, technologies like **Silver Lining** (http://cloudsilverlining.org/) may enable one-click deployments. In fact, this is possible today with some Python-based (and other) frameworks and hosting providers, like **Pylons** and **Rackspace Cloud**, respectively.

Unfortunately in Plone's case, this technology is not so common as to have made it into this book. It may be closer to reality on **Amazon EC2**; visit the link http://www.slideshare.net/Jazkarta/plone-in-the-cloud-an-ondemand-cms-hosted-on-amazon-ec2.

In the meantime, checking in your Plone buildouts (and add-on package source code) to Subversion (or a version control system of your choice) is a reasonable approach to help manage the tasks at hand, which brings us back to this chapter.

By now:

- In theory, we have checked out the buildout to staging and production, and have automated various maintenance tasks
- In practice, we may have already performed various optimization tasks too, though we are just now getting to them here

In this chapter, you will learn:

- About caching in the context of Plone
- Installing **CacheFu**—a caching add-on for Plone
- Installing **Varnish**—a caching agent
- Installing **Squid**—a caching agent
- About load balancing in the context of Plone
- Using Buildout macros to create multiple Zope 2 instances
- Installing **HAProxy**—a load balancer
- Installing **Pound**—a load balancer
- Installing **Supervisor**—a process manager
- Understanding the software stack
- Installing **Munin** plugins to analyze performance

Windows folks, consider your options

It may be more difficult to follow along here, as various technologies become more difficult to install and configure, or may not work at all on Windows.

Our apologies!

In the case of a caching agent, you may find that Squid is better supported than Varnish; visit http://wiki.squid-cache.org/SquidFaq/ BinaryPackages#Windows for more information.

Because Supervisor does not work on Windows, you can use Windows services to achieve the same effect (which is what the Plone installer for Windows does for you).

If everything else fails, you may seek help from the good folks at Enfold Systems, and perhaps experiment with some of their software like Enfold Server: http://www.enfoldsystems.com/software/server/.

Alternatively, we suggest an Ubuntu Linux virtual machine, running on the freely available VirtualBox (http://www.virtualbox.org/wiki/ Downloads).

Caching background in the context of Plone

Zope 2 is an application server. Therefore, every page it delivers involves "doing work", which results in server and network load. If possible, to conserve the system resources, you may want to cache your site's content as much as is practical and possible.

Caching agents store resources needed to serve the site's content and answer site requests with these resources, until the browser or caching agent is no longer able to do so (for example, when a caching rule tells the browser or caching agent that the page has expired).

At this point, it must contact the application server again for new data.

Installing CacheFu—a caching add-on for Plone

Traditionally, the very first thing many people do to improve Plone's performance is install the CacheFu add-on product.

CacheFu has been around since the Plone 2.5.x days, and has been a welcome addition for folks trying to improve the performance of an increasingly complex and slower running software stack.

Although it is not the magic elixir that many hope it to be, it does provide a decent, measurable improvement for very little effort; so it is usually a good idea to explore.

It does this by creating and configuring several cache-related Zope objects such as **RAMCacheManager** with a reasonable set of defaults. CacheFu saves you from having to learn and fully understand the necessary Zope 2 concepts needed to be able to create and configure these objects by hand. It also saves you from having to know about complex web caching, in general. You should probably learn these things too, but you don't have to learn them now.

The addition of CacheFu alone can provide a better performance, but a lot more so when it is combined with a caching agent like Varnish or Squid. We will get to caching agents later in this chapter.

For the next section, we will focus primarily on adding CacheFu to our buildout, and getting it installed and running properly.

About CacheFu

CacheFu is covered in much more detail in *"Practical Plone 3"*, *Packt Publishing* (https://www.packtpub.com/practical-plone-3-beginners-guide-to-building-powerful-websites/book). However, you should be aware that it is beginning to show its age.

If you are interested in the next generation caching add-on for Plone, please check out **plone.app.caching** on http://pypi.python.org/pypi/plone.app.caching, currently in the alpha release. Watch out for a beta release in the middle of 2010 (around the time this book is published).

In `06-deployment-optimization-cachefu.cfg`, we have the following:

```
[buildout]
extends = 05-deployment-maintenance-rotate2.cfg

[instance]
eggs += Products.CacheSetup
```

Now, run Buildout:

```
$ bin/buildout -c 06-deployment-optimization-cachefu.cfg
```

You should see:

```
$ bin/buildout -c 06-deployment-optimization-cachefu.cfg
...
Getting distribution for 'Products.CacheSetup'.
  File "build/bdist.macosx-10.6-i386/egg/Products/CacheSetup/skins/cache_setup/cache_policy_redirect.py", line 15
    return ct.setDisplayPolicy(policy_id, camefrom=camefrom,
redirect=True)
SyntaxError: 'return' outside function
...
Got Products.CacheSetup 1.2.1.
Getting distribution for 'Products.PolicyHTTPCacheManager'.
Got Products.PolicyHTTPCacheManager 1.2.
Getting distribution for 'Products.PageCacheManager'.
Got Products.PageCacheManager 1.2.
Getting distribution for 'Products.CMFSquidTool'.
Got Products.CMFSquidTool 1.5.1.
...
```

SyntaxErrors are not "real"

Remember that the syntax errors above are not "real" errors. They are caused by Distribute trying to compile Zope 2 script (Python) files located on the filesystem into byte code (because they end with `.py`). However, Zope 2 uses these files when publishing objects to the Web, so compiling these makes no sense.

Typically, these scripts are found in directories called as Filesystem Directory Views, which are used by CMF Skin Layers. For more information about Zope 2 script (Python) objects, please visit `http://docs.zope.org/zope2/zope2book/BasicScripting.html#creating-python-based-scripts`.

For more information about why you can ignore these errors, refer to *Chapter 2, Site Basics* of this book.

Now start Plone:

```
$ bin/instance fg
```

To install CacheFu, browse to `http://localhost:8080/Plone` and click on **Site Setup | Add-on Products**. You should see:

Select the box next to **CacheSetup 1.2.1.jarn.2** and click on **Install**.

Once installed, click on the **Cache Configuration Tool** in the **Add-on Product Configuration** section.

To enable CacheFu, check the **Enable CacheFu** box and click on **Save**:

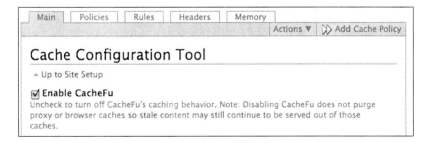

You should experience a significant performance improvement as a result.

For example with CacheFu enabled, using a server-benchmarking tool like **ab** (`http://httpd.apache.org/docs/2.2/programs/ab.html`) you may experience serving approximately 80 requests per second:

```
$ ab -c 1 -n 100 http://127.0.0.1:8080/Plone/
This is ApacheBench, Version 2.3 <$Revision: 655654 $>
Copyright 1996 Adam Twiss, Zeus Technology Ltd, http://www.zeustech.net/
Licensed to The Apache Software Foundation, http://www.apache.org/
Benchmarking 127.0.0.1 (be patient).....done
...
Requests per second:    80.08 [#/sec] (mean)
...
```

Now disable CacheFu (uncheck the **Enable CacheFu** box and click on **Save)**.

At this point, you may experience serving only approximately 10 requests per second:

```
$ ab -c 1 -n 100 http://127.0.0.1:8080/Plone/
This is ApacheBench, Version 2.3 <$Revision: 655654 $>
Copyright 1996 Adam Twiss, Zeus Technology Ltd, http://www.zeustech.net/
Licensed to The Apache Software Foundation, http://www.apache.org/
Benchmarking 127.0.0.1 (be patient).....done
...
Requests per second:    10.19 [#/sec] (mean)
...
```

It is not the exact numbers that are important here, just the variation in results.

You can also use the Firefox add-on **Live HTTP Headers** (`http://livehttpheaders.mozdev.org/`) to examine the HTTP headers.

To do so:

1. Download Live HTTP Headers from `http://livehttpheaders.mozdev.org/` and install it in Firefox.
2. Select **Tools | Live HTTP Headers**.
3. Browse to `http://localhost:8080/Plone`.

You should see:

```
http://localhost:8080/Plone
GET /Plone HTTP/1.1
Host: localhost:8080
User-Agent: Mozilla/5.0 (Macintosh; U; Intel Mac OS X 10.6; en-US;
rv:1.9.2.3) Gecko/20100401 Firefox/3.6.3
...
X-Cache-Headers-Set-By: CachingPolicyManager: /Plone/caching_policy_
manager
Expires: Tue, 23 May 2000 13:09:40 GMT
Vary: Accept-Encoding
Etag: |admin|Plone Default|en-us;en;q=0.5|1|159||||354013
X-Caching-Rule-Id: plone-content-types
Cache-Control: max-age=0, s-maxage=0, private, must-revalidate
```

In particular, you will notice the caching-related headers like `Cache-Control`, `Etag`, `Vary`, and so on.

At this point, we have done nothing but install CacheFu. We are still serving our site directly from Zope 2.

In production, we would most likely deploy this site behind Apache or Nginx, inside a virtual host that would proxy/rewrite requests to Zope 2. A Zope 2 deployment proxied by Apache or Nginx is fine for many sites, but some sites require more.

So let us now add a caching agent *between* the web server and Zope 2 to help improve caching even more (of course, we have not actually added the frontend web server yet).

We have a couple of options when it comes to adding a caching agent. We will begin by covering the state-of-the-art, high-performance HTTP accelerator Varnish followed by the venerable Squid caching proxy for the Web.

Installing Varnish—a caching agent

To add Varnish to your Buildout, you can use one of the CMMI recipes (`configure;` `make; make install`) like **zc.recipe.cmmi** (`http://pypi.python.org/pypi/` `zc.recipe.cmmi`) or **hexagonit.recipe.cmmi** (`http://pypi.python.org/pypi/` `hexagonit.recipe.cmmi`).

You can also use an operating system vendor package. Whichever you choose, you may want to use Buildout to create a Varnish configuration file suitable to use with your Plone site.

Advanced users may create their own configuration file template, and generate a configuration file dynamically when Buildout runs, with the help of the **collective. recipe.template** recipe (`http://pypi.python.org/pypi/collective.recipe. template`).

We will not cover installation with vendor packages, or the advanced template generation approach.

What we *will* cover is Varnish installation and configuration with zc.recipe.cmmi (`http://pypi.python.org/pypi/zc.recipe.cmmi`) and **plone.recipe.varnish** (`http://pypi.python.org/pypi/plone.recipe.varnish`).

Which CMMI recipe should I use?

CMMI stands for `configure; make; make install`, which are a set of UNIX commands typically used to install software from source code distributions (based on conventions set by the `autoconf/automake/ libtool` developer tools).

Take a look at the various features provided by each, described on `http://pypi.python.org/pypi/zc.recipe.cmmi` and `http:// pypi.python.org/pypi/hexagonit.recipe.cmmi`.

The former provides basic CMMI functionality, with some advanced features like setting environment variables.

The latter provides a few more advanced features, like pre and post-make hooks to allow you to execute arbitrary commands in addition to running `configure; make; make install`.

In `06-deployment-optimization-varnish.cfg`, we have:

```
[buildout]
extends = 06-deployment-optimization-cachefu.cfg
parts +=
    varnish-install
    varnish

[varnish-install]
recipe = zc.recipe.cmmi
url = http://downloads.sourceforge.net/project/varnish/varnish/2.1.2/\
  varnish-2.1.2.tar.gz
```

```
[varnish]
recipe = plone.recipe.varnish
daemon = ${varnish-install:location}/sbin/varnishd
```

Now run Buildout:

```
$ bin/buildout -c 06-deployment-optimization-varnish.cfg
```

You should see:

```
$ bin/buildout -c 06-deployment-optimization-varnish.cfg

...

Installing varnish-install.

varnish-install: Downloading http://downloads.sourceforge.net/project/
varnish/varnish/2.1.2/varnish-2.1.2.tar.gz

varnish-install: Unpacking and configuring

...

Installing varnish
```

Now start Varnish with:

```
$ bin/varnish -F
```

Browse to `http://localhost:8000/Plone`. (Note that the port in this URL is 8000.)

Assuming your ZEO and Zope 2 instances are running, you should now see your Plone site (because the default Varnish configuration binds to port 8000 and proxies to port 8080).

If you do not see your Plone site, you may want stop everything and restart as follows:

```
$ bin/zeo start
```
```
$ bin/instance start
```
```
$ bin/varnish -F
```

In this way, we have configured ZEO and Plone to run in the background, while Varnish is running in the foreground (thanks to -F).

You can always check the status of ZEO and Plone with the status command.

In the case of ZEO, you should see:

```
$ bin/zeo status
program running; pid=1088
```

In the case of Plone, you should see:

```
$ bin/instance status
program running; pid=10944
```

That takes care of Varnish. Now let us move on to Squid.

Installing Squid—a caching agent

To install squid, we will use the zc.recipe.cmmi recipe (`http://pypi.python.org/pypi/zc.recipe.cmmi`) and **plone.recipe.squid** recipe (`http://pypi.python.org/pypi/plone.recipe.squid`).

In `06-deployment-optimization-squid.cfg`, we have:

```
[buildout]
extends = 06-deployment-optimization-varnish.cfg
parts +=
    squid-install
    squid

[squid-install]
recipe = zc.recipe.cmmi
url = http://www.squid-cache.org/Versions/v3/3.0/\
  squid-3.0.STABLE21.tar.gz

[squid]
recipe = plone.recipe.squid:instance
cache-size = 1000
daemon = ${squid-install:location}/sbin/squid
backends = 127.0.0.1:8080
bind = 127.0.0.1:3128
```

Now stop Varnish and run Buildout:

```
$ bin/buildout -c 06-deployment-optimization-squid.cfg
```

Next, be sure to create some cache swap directories for Squid, with the following command:

```
$ bin/squid -z
```

You should see:

```
$ bin/squid -z
2010/05/21 11:54:41| Creating Swap Directories
```

Next, start Squid in the foreground (with -N), as shown:

```
$ bin/squid -N
```

Now, browse to `http://localhost:3128/Plone`. (Note that the port in this URL is 3128.)

Assuming your ZEO and Zope 2 instances are running, you should now see your Plone site (because the default Squid configuration binds to port 3128 and proxies to port 8080).

At this point, we should take a minute to explain the direction we are heading in.

We have configured various caching agents in front of Plone, as well as configured Plone to be more cache-aware via CacheFu.

The next step to improve performance is to divide the application server work amongst one or more Zope 2 instances, assuming of course you have the appropriate hardware to handle such a configuration.

Choosing the right number of instances

For more information about choosing the appropriate number of Zope 2 instances for your hardware configuration, see Elizabeth Leddy's *awesome* Plone Conference 2009 presentation Unloading Plone.

Visit `http://www.slideshare.net/eleddy/unloading-plone` for the slides and `http://plone.blip.tv/file/3042000/` for the video.

This process will leave you with two or more instances running on various ports.

But you will need a way to aggregate traffic, and direct it in a sane way to the various idle instances waiting to serve you.

This is similar to the checkout line of a grocery store, where instead of having your choice of lines, you are directed through a single line first then arbitrarily (or sequentially) directed to one of the cashiers (who may or may not have a bagger).

In this way, everyone gets a fair turn and your grocery store (or website) performs much better.

To create multiple instances, we will use Buildout macros.

Creating multiple instances with Buildout macros

As of version 1.4 of zc.buildout, it is possible to extend sections (except for the buildout section) with the use of the special < parameter. So, to create a macro, create a section with whatever you parameters you want in it, for example foo:

```
[foo]
bar = baz
```

Then create another section or sections such as foo1 and foo2 and set the < parameter with the value of the section you want to copy:

```
[foo1]
< = foo

[foo2]
< = foo
```

So foo1 and foo2 now contain:

```
bar = baz
```

You can now override and add whatever parameters you like:

```
[foo3]
< = foo
# bar gets bilge, instead of baz
bar = bilge
# car gets baz
car = ${foo:bar}
```

And so on.

That means we can now define a base instance section (which we did in buildout. cfg) and use it as a macro to create additional instance sections.

To demonstrate this, we will create two additional instances, based on the instance section in buildout.cfg.

In 06-deployment-optimization-macros.cfg, we have:

```
[buildout]
extends = 06-deployment-optimization-squid.cfg
parts +=

    instance1
    instance2
[instance1]
< = instance
http-address = 8081

[instance2]
< = instance
http-address = 8082
```

You should be aware that by doing this, we inherit various settings from the instance section in buildout.cfg, and then change the http-address parameter for each new instance.

Now run buildout with:

```
$ bin/buildout -c 06-deployment-optimization-macros.cfg
```

You should see:

```
$ bin/buildout -c 06-deployment-optimization-macros.cfg

...

Installing instance1.
Generated script '/Users/aclark/Developer/plone-site-admin/buildout/bin/
instance1'.
Installing instance2.
Generated script '/Users/aclark/Developer/plone-site-admin/buildout/bin/
instance2'.
```

Of course at this point to run our Plone site, we have to start four different services, for example:

```
$ bin/zeo start
$ bin/instance1 start
$ bin/instance2 start
$ bin/varnish
```

Also, we have not yet aggregated the instance traffic.

We will address these two problems next, starting with load balancing.

Load balancing in the context of Plone

Load balancing (in the Plone context) is the process of distributing requests amongst two or more Zope 2 instances, capable of handling the load. There are a variety of tools available to help with load balancing in Plone including Apache, Varnish, HAProxy, and Pound.

Of these, we will focus primarily on HAProxy and Pound, as they provide the most full-featured and flexible implementations.

Installing HAProxy—a load balancer

One popular load balancer is HAProxy (`http://haproxy.1wt.eu/`).

You may reach for it when you would like a more fully-featured load balancer than Pound (covered a little later, not to impugn Pound's work).

The HAProxy binary

To make installation with Buildout easy, there is a recipe called **plone.recipe. haproxy** (`http://pypi.python.org/pypi/plone.recipe.haproxy`).

In `06-deployment-optimization-haproxy.cfg`, we have:

```
[buildout]
extends = 06-deployment-optimization-macros.cfg
parts +=
    haproxy-install

[haproxy-install]
recipe = plone.recipe.haproxy
```

Firstly, you will notice that the source URL is configured by default to `http://dist. plone.org/thirdparty/haproxy-1.4.4.zip` which you can override if you like, as shown:

```
[haproxy-install]
recipe = plone.recipe.haproxy
url = http://my.dist.server/haproxy-1.4.4.zip
```

Secondly, you will also notice that we did not use any CMMI recipe, due to the fact that the package does not follow the CMMI standard (`configure; make; make install`). Therefore, this recipe is a workaround.

You will also notice that we did not use the author's `.tar.gz` distribution (available here: `http://haproxy.1wt.eu/download/1.4/src/haproxy-1.4.6.tar.gz`) due to some difficulties encountered during untar/ungzip.

Now run buildout:

```
$ bin/buildout -c 06-deployment-optimization-haproxy.cfg
```

You should see:

```
Getting distribution for 'plone.recipe.haproxy'.

Got plone.recipe.haproxy 1.1.

...

haproxy-install: Adding script wrapper for haproxy
```

The HAProxy configuration file

Unfortunately, this recipe does not generate a configuration file for us; neither does **plone.recipe.pound** (`http://pypi.python.org/pypi/plone.recipe.pound`).

Others such as **isotoma.recipe.pound** (`http://pypi.python.org/pypi/isotoma.recipe.pound`) generate a configuration file.

In the case of application-specific recipes that do not generate configuration files, this is not necessarily a drawback as some folks prefer more control, or more features than the application-specific recipes (for example, Varnish, Pound, and so on) can provide.

Another common complaint filed against the application-specific recipes, is that they provide too much complexity, and too many layers of indirection.

So let us take this opportunity to demonstrate the ultimate in a simple configuration file generation with flexibility with the help collective.recipe.template (`http://pypi.python.org/pypi/collective.recipe.template`).

In the book examples, you will find a templates directory that contains two files:

- `haproxy.conf.in`
- `pound.conf.in`

Each of these files contains sample configuration in comments, followed by simple configurations designed to work with Plone.

In `06-deployment-optimization-haproxy-config.cfg`, we have:

```
[buildout]
extends = 06-deployment-optimization-haproxy.cfg
parts +=
    haproxy-config

[haproxy-config]
recipe = collective.recipe.template
input = ${buildout:directory}/templates/haproxy.cfg.in
output = ${buildout:directory}/etc/haproxy.cfg
```

You will notice that in the `haproxy-config` section we tell collective.recipe.template about its `input` and `output` files.

The `input` template's variable substitution syntax is the same as Buildout's — very simple.

So, if you want to refer to the buildout directory in a configuration file, you can use:

`${buildout:directory}`

One word of warning — comments will not stop collective.recipe.template from trying to substitute variables (although it might be nice if they did).

Now, anytime you want to edit HAProxy's configuration, you should edit `templates/haproxy.cfg.in` and run Buildout.

This will produce a "real" configuration file in `etc/haproxy.cfg`, which you can use to run HAProxy, like this:

`$ bin/haproxy -f etc/haproxy.cfg`

Now run Buildout:

`$ bin/buildout -c 06-deployment-optimization-haproxy-config.cfg`

You should see:

`$ bin/buildout -c 06-deployment-optimization-haproxy-config.cfg`

`...`

`Installing haproxy-config.`

Now you can run HAProxy as shown:

`$ bin/haproxy -f etc/haproxy.cfg`

And browse to `http://localhost:10000/Plone`.

Assuming your ZEO and Zope 2 instances are running, you should now see your Plone site (based on the configuration in `etc/haproxy.cfg`).

Installing Pound—a load balancer

Another popular load balancer is Pound (`http://www.apsis.ch/pound/`).

Instead of using plone.recipe.pound, we will try a simpler more generic approach with hexagonit.recipe.cmmi.

The Pound binary

In `06-deployment-optimization-pound.cfg`, we have:

```
[buildout]
extends = 06-deployment-optimization-haproxy-config.cfg
parts =
    pound-install

[pound-install]
recipe = hexagonit.recipe.cmmi
url = http://www.apsis.ch/pound/Pound-2.4.5.tgz
make-targets =
keep-compile-dir = true
```

Here, you will notice we have configured an empty value for the `make-targets` parameter. That is because we do not want to configure any `make-targets`. Normally, the `make-targets` include `make`; `make install`, but we do not want to call `make install` because it tries to change ownership of files to the daemon user which every system does not have:

```
make-targets =
```

Instead, we will use the binary in the installation, which we leave in place with:

```
keep-compile-dir = true
```

You can verify that Pound has been installed with the following command:

```
$ ls ./parts/pound-install__compile__/Pound-2.4.5/pound
```

You should see:

```
$ ls ./parts/pound-install__compile__/Pound-2.4.5/pound
./parts/pound-install__compile__/Pound-2.4.5/pound*
```

The Pound configuration file

To create a configuration file we can use with Pound, we will again use collective. recipe.template (`http://pypi.python.org/pypi/collective.recipe.template`).

In `06-deployment-optimization-pound-config.cfg`, you should see:

```
[buildout]
extends = 06-deployment-optimization-pound.cfg
parts += pound-config

[pound-config]
recipe = collective.recipe.template
input = ${buildout:directory}/templates/pound.cfg.in
output = ${buildout:directory}/etc/pound.cfg
```

We know from our previous experience how collective.recipe.template uses `templates/pound.cfg.in` to produce `etc/pound.cfg`.

Now start Pound with:

```
$ ./parts/pound-install__compile__/Pound-2.4.5/pound -f etc/pound.cfg
```

And browse to `http://localhost:10001/Plone`.

Assuming your ZEO and Zope 2 instances are running, you should now see your Plone site (based on the configuration in `etc/pound.cfg`).

Installing Supervisor—a process manager

We have begun to accumulate quite a few of programs in our software stack.

In order to facilitate easy and consistent operation of these programs, we can use an excellent tool called Supervisor (`http://supervisord.org`) to help us.

As it so happens, there is a Buildout recipe to make configuration file generation easy called **collective.recipe.supervisor** (`http://pypi.python.org/pypi/collective.recipe.supervisor`). This one is too easy and simple to resist (hence its popularity).

In `06-deployment-optimization-supervisor.cfg`, we have:

```
[buildout]
extends = 06-deployment-optimization-pound-config.cfg
parts += supervisor
```

```
[pound]
directory = ${buildout:directory}/parts/pound-install__compile__

[supervisor]
recipe = collective.recipe.supervisor
programs =
#Prio    Name        Program                                    Params
  00       zeo         ${zeo:location}/bin/runzeo
  00       instance1   ${instance1:location}/bin/runzope
  00       instance2   ${instance2:location}/bin/runzope
  00       haproxy     ${buildout:directory}/bin/haproxy      \
     [-f etc/haproxy.cfg]
  00         pound     ${pound:directory}/Pound-2.4.5/pound \
     [-f etc/pound.cfg]
  00       varnish     ${buildout:directory}/bin/varnish      [-F]
  00       squid       ${buildout:directory}/bin/squid        [-N]
```

We use the pound section to make the path to Pound installation a little more manageable. And we use the programs parameter in the supervisor section to tell Supervisor which programs to run.

You will notice that the priority is set to zero for all of the programs. That is because according to the author Chris McDonough (http://plope.com), the priority setting in Supervisor does not behave as expected.

So when in doubt, you can just give all the programs the same priority.

Now run Buildout:

```
$ bin/buildout -c 06-deployment-optimization-supervisor.cfg
```

You should see:

```
$ bin/buildout -c 06-deployment-optimization-supervisor.cfg

...

Installing supervisor.
Generated script '/Users/aclark/Developer/plone-site-admin/buildout/bin/
supervisord'.
Generated script '/Users/aclark/Developer/plone-site-admin/buildout/bin/
supervisorctl'.
```

This configures the entire stack to run all at once; of course, we probably do not need two load balancers and two caching agents.

To check if everything is in order, you can run this command:

```
$ bin/supervisord -e debug -n
```

You should see:

```
$ bin/supervisord -e debug -n

...

2010-05-21 19:03:04,652 INFO supervisord started with pid 19129
2010-05-21 19:03:05,654 INFO spawned: 'haproxy' with pid 19131
2010-05-21 19:03:05,657 INFO spawned: 'varnish' with pid 19132
2010-05-21 19:03:05,660 INFO spawned: 'pound' with pid 19133
2010-05-21 19:03:05,677 INFO spawned: 'squid' with pid 19134
2010-05-21 19:03:05,682 INFO spawned: 'zeo' with pid 19135
2010-05-21 19:03:05,707 INFO spawned: 'instance2' with pid 19136
2010-05-21 19:03:05,723 INFO spawned: 'instance1' with pid 19140
2010-05-21 19:03:05,724 DEBG fd 10 closed, stopped monitoring

...

2010-05-21 19:03:06,954 INFO spawned: 'haproxy' with pid 19150
2010-05-21 19:03:06,955 INFO success: varnish entered RUNNING state,
process has stayed up for > than 1 seconds (startsecs)
2010-05-21 19:03:06,955 INFO success: pound entered RUNNING state,
process has stayed up for > than 1 seconds (startsecs)
2010-05-21 19:03:06,955 INFO success: squid entered RUNNING state,
process has stayed up for > than 1 seconds (startsecs)
2010-05-21 19:03:06,955 INFO success: zeo entered RUNNING state, process
has stayed up for > than 1 seconds (startsecs)
2010-05-21 19:03:06,956 INFO success: instance2 entered RUNNING state,
process has stayed up for > than 1 seconds (startsecs)
2010-05-21 19:03:06,956 INFO success: instance1 entered RUNNING state,
process has stayed up for > than 1 seconds (startsecs)
```

It should stay that way. If there are any problems, you will see them immediately.

This chapter has been a mouthful, but there is still more to go!

In order to put the finishing touches on the optimization chapter, we need to take a look at how to figure what parts of our site need optimizing.

One way to do that is to use Munin, using the Munin plugins for Zope 2 and Plone.

With this impressive program, you can easily create beautiful graphs of Zope 2 and Plone performance data.

Understanding the software stack

First, let's review the complex software stack we have created in this chapter.

This is just one of the many scenarios you could deploy within production to handle various types of production environments you may encounter.

Our stack currently looks like this:

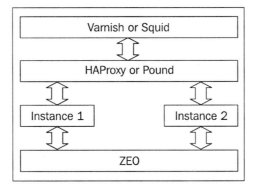

In production, it may look like this:

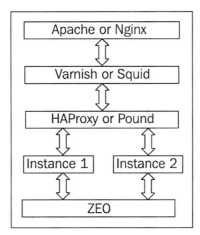

That is to say that in production, you may place a web server like Apache or Nginx in front (on port 80), and then proxy requests to the web server to a web cache like Varnish or Squid, which may then proxy requests down the stack to the Zope 2 instances as needed.

Frontend Apache configuration

In Apache, the proxy configuration typically looks like this (assuming mod_rewrite and mod_proxy have been loaded):

```
RewriteEngine On
RewriteRule ^(.*) http://127.0.0.1:8080/VirtualHostBase/http/mysite.
com:80/Plone/\
   VirtualHostRoot/$1 [P,L]
```

You will typically find these entries inside a **VirtualHost** container (but not always).

Frontend Nginx configuration

In Nginx, it typically looks like this:

```
proxy_pass http://localhost:8080/VirtualHostBase/http/mysite.com:80/
Plone/\
   VirtualHostRoot/;
```

You will typically find these entries inside a server { location / { } } block (but not always).

In both of these cases, you may typically rely on the operating system vendor packages to install the frontend Apache or Nginx.

Please note that this is only one of many possible production deployment scenarios. The right way to deploy is a decision you must make, based on the details of each production environment.

We will leave these things to the professionals—you, or your system administrator.

Now, we get back to Munin.

Installing Munin plugins to analyze performance

As we mentioned earlier, Munin produces graphs that contain diagnostic system information.

With Zope 2, you can analyze four different parameters over time:

- Memory
- Cache
- Threads
- ZODB

To create graphs with Munin, you must install the Munin plugins in Zope 2 as well as install the Munin software on your production server (that is, outside the buildout).

Munin installation should be fairly trivial on most UNIX-like operating systems, including our target operating system Ubuntu Linux. Munin software is typically bundled into three separate packages—**munin**, **munin-node**, and **munin-plugins**.

Assuming you have one server, you should have at least the munin and munin-node packages installed to facilitate monitoring of that server and the Plone site running on it.

If you have more than one server (running Plone), you should add munin-nodes to each additional server and configure them to be nodes of the server with the munin package installed.

To install the Munin plugins in Zope 2, we will use the **munin.zope** package (http://pypi.python.org/pypi/munin.zope/).

Installing the munin.zope package

This package can be a little confusing to install, but the process is relatively simple once you understand that the installation creates a bin/munin script to do two things:

- Create symbolic links from the Munin plugins directory to the bin/munin script
- Produce input for Munin when invoked via the symbolic link

In 06-deployment-optimization-munin.cfg, we have:

```
[buildout]
extends = 06-deployment-optimization-supervisor.cfg
parts += munin

[instance]
eggs += munin.zope
zcml += munin.zope

[munin]
recipe = zc.recipe.egg
eggs = munin.zope
arguments = http_address='${instance:http-address}',\
    user='${instance:user}'
```

You will notice we pass the HTTP address and credentials to log in to our Plone site, in the arguments parameter.

You will also notice we use the zc.recipe.egg recipe (`http://pypi.python.org/pypi/zc.recipe.egg`) to create a `bin/munin` script.

Now run Buildout:

```
$ bin/buildout -c 06-deployment-optimization-munin.cfg
```

Now start ZEO:

```
$ bin/zeo
```

And start Plone:

```
$ bin/instance fg
```

Testing the munin.zope plugins through the Web

After logging in (via `http://localhost:8080/manage`), browse to `http://localhost:8080/@@munin.zope.plugins/zopememory` and you should see (something like):

Next, browse to `http://localhost:8080/@@munin.zope.plugins/zopethreads` and you should see (something like):

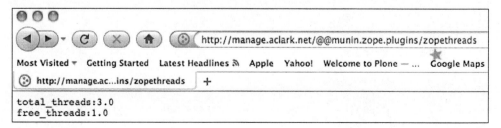

After that, browse to `http://localhost:8080/@@munin.zope.plugins/zopecache` and you should see (something like):

Finally, browse to `http://localhost:8080/@@munin.zope.plugins/ zodbactivity` and you should see (something like):

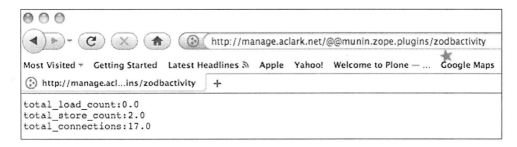

Installing the munin.zope plugins on the command line

At this point, the Zope 2 instance is configured properly, but Munin knows nothing about the Zope 2 instance.

To configure the plugins for use in Munin, run `bin/munin` on your production server with the `install` command and the location of the `plug-ins` directory, as following:

```
$ sudo bin/munin install /etc/munin/plugins
```

You should see:

```
$ sudo bin/munin install /etc/munin/plugins

installed symlink /etc/munin/plugins/aclark_zopecache_aclark

installed symlink /etc/munin/plugins/aclark_zopememory_aclark

installed symlink /etc/munin/plugins/aclark_zodbactivity_aclark

installed symlink /etc/munin/plugins/aclark_zopethreads_aclark
```

Testing the munin.zope plugins on the command line

You can also test the plugins on the command line, as shown:

```
$ /etc/munin/plugins/aclark_zopecache_aclark
Total_objects_in_database.value 22959.0
Total_objects_in_all_caches.value 3867.0
Target_number_to_cache.value 20000.0

$ /etc/munin/plugins/aclark_zopememory_aclark
VmPeak.value 495312896.0
VmSize.value 429277184.0
VmLck.value 0.0
VmHWM.value 140443648.0
VmRSS.value 75329536.0
VmData.value 226422784.0
VmStk.value 405504.0
VmExe.value 1392640.0
VmLib.value 10489856.0
VmPTE.value 704512.0

$ /etc/munin/plugins/aclark_zopecache_aclark
Total_objects_in_database.value 22959.0
Total_objects_in_all_caches.value 3867.0
Target_number_to_cache.value 20000.0

$ /etc/munin/plugins/aclark_zopethreads_aclark
Total_threads.value 3.0
Free_threads.value 1.0
aclark@aclark:~/ > /etc/munin/plugins/aclark_zodbactivity_aclark
Total_objects_loaded.value 0.0
Total_objects_stored.value 0.0
Total_connections.value 11.0
```

After five minutes (the default length of time between Munin runs), check your Munin web directory, for example /var/www/munin for images and HTML files.

Munin graphs

Now let us take a look at some sample data (from the author's server). What follows is a selection of the most interesting graphs chosen from the day, month, week, and year graphs for each plugin.

ZODB activity

The following graph shows a correlation between total connections and total objects loaded, perhaps indicating that most connections reference the same set of objects:

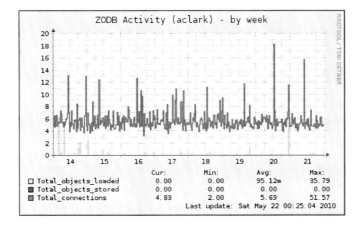

Zope cache parameters

The next graph shows a correlation between the total number of objects in the database, the target number of objects to cache, and the total objects in all caches, perhaps indicating that the target number of objects to cache should be set higher:

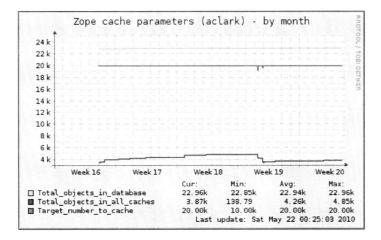

Zope memory usage

The next graph shows a correlation between various memory usage statistics and is perhaps the most interesting of the group:

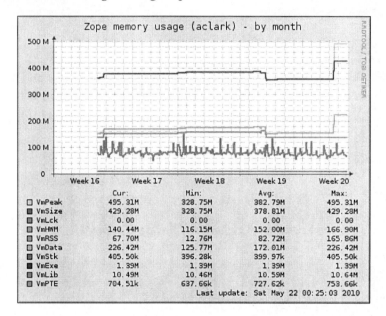

In particular, the point where **VmPeak** rose above **VmSize**, perhaps indicates that more memory is needed.

Zope 2 server threads

The last graph shows a correlation between total threads and free threads, apparently indicating that three out of four threads are in use most of the time:

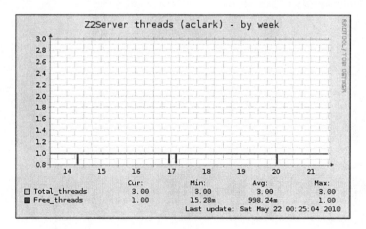

These graphs are at the very least interesting, and at the most can be invaluable when you are experiencing performance-related issues and you do not know the cause.

In addition to munin.zope, there are two more potentially useful plugin packages you may wish to experiment with:

- `http://pypi.python.org/pypi/munin.plone`
- `http://pypi.python.org/pypi/munin.varnish`

Summary

In this chapter, you have learned:

- Web caching, particularly as it relates to Plone
- How to install CacheFu in Plone to configure cache settings
- How to add Varnish and Squid to your buildout to use as caching agents
- Load balancing, particularly as it relates to Plone
- How to use the < parameter in Buildout to create macros
- How to add HAProxy and Pound to your buildout to do load balancing
- How to add Supervisor to your buildout to manage processes
- How the production stack works
- How to add Munin plugins to your buildout

See you in Chapter 7, where we will adjust and configure various security-related settings.

7
Security

While Plone is quite fortunate to be built on top of the very safe and secure Zope 2 application server, there is always more we can do to make sure our site is running as safely and securely as possible.

Because security is such a big topic, there are many areas where we can perform audits and make improvements such as operating system (OS), filesystem (FS), through the web (TTW), and so on.

Lastly, there are some miscellaneous tasks that fall under the security umbrella; we can take this opportunity to learn them.

So let's get to it.

In this chapter, you will learn:

- Restricting TCP/IP access to localhost or LAN host
- Managing IP addresses and ports effectively
- Configuring the Zope 2 effective user dynamically
- Installing **Cassandra** to audit through the web (TTW) security
- Applying security and bug fixes to Plone

More about security

For a closer look at a variety of Plone-related security information, visit http://plone.org/products/plone/security/overview.

For Erik Rose and Steve McMahon's excellent Plone Conference 2008 talk, visit http://plone.org/events/conferences/2008-washington-dc/agenda/securing-zope-and-plone-against-the-big-bad-internet/.

Restricting TCP/IP access to localhost or LAN host

One of the simplest things we can do to secure our system is to operate our Zope 2 instances only on the IP addresses that they are required to listen on.

In most cases, it is 127.0.0.1 (or localhost, as it is commonly referred to) but it can also be a LAN host that is a private, non-routable IP address used only on your local area network (LAN).

In this chapter, we will not cover LAN hosts. However, we suggest you consider using them when you need to access instances from another host on the LAN; otherwise, just use localhost.

In the case of LAN hosts, once configured, they will protect ports from being accessed by the outside world (that is Internet). However, it will allow them to be accessible from the LAN where you may want to configure monitoring, for example via Munin (covered in Chapter 6), **Zenoss** (http://community.zenoss.org), and so on.

What we will cover is how to use the localhost IP address.

In 07-security-localhost.cfg, we have:

```
[buildout]
extends = 06-deployment-optimization-munin.cfg

[instance1]
http-address = 127.0.0.1:8081

[instance2]
http-address = 127.0.0.1:8082
```

You will notice we have re-configured the http-address parameter to include the entire HTTP address and not just the port number.

You will also notice we have used the private, non-routable localhost address 127.0.0.1.

Now run Buildout:

```
$ bin/buildout -c 07-security-localhost.cfg
```

Afterward, in `parts/instance1/etc/zope.conf`, you should see:

```
...
<http-server>
  # valid keys are "address" and "force-connection-close"
  address 127.0.0.1:8081
  # force-connection-close on
  # You can also use the WSGI interface between ZServer and
ZPublisher:
  # use-wsgi on

</http-server>
```

This means that our instances will listen for connections only on 127.0.0.1; any attempt to connect from another host will fail.

> **More about localhost**
>
> For more information about how the localhost really works, visit `http://en.wikipedia.org/wiki/Localhost`. For our purpose though, we can think of running the Plone site on localhost as "having a party that only your laptop or development workstation can join".

Managing IP addresses and ports effectively

As your production configuration grows, it may become more difficult to manage a large number of IP addresses and ports.

As such, it is often helpful to have them defined in their own section.

In `07-security-ports.cfg`, we have:

```
[buildout]
extends = 07-security-localhost.cfg

[hosts]
localhost = 127.0.0.1

[ports]
instance1 = 8081
instance2 = 8082
```

Notice that we are not using these definitions for anything yet. But we can use them like this:

```
${hosts:localhost}:${ports:instance1}
${hosts:localhost}:${ports:instance2}
```

Effectively from now on, we have to change IP addresses and port numbers only in one place (assuming we change all static references such as `127.0.0.1:8080` to the new syntax).

Configuring the Zope 2 effective user dynamically

Another simple thing we can do to secure our system is to operate our Zope 2 instances with only those operating system users who have enough permission to execute the instances. In fact, Zope 2 will not run as root on UNIX-like systems.

However, we frequently forget to do this. More importantly, sometimes we want to be more explicit with our configuration. This is where the `effective-user` parameter comes in handy. If no effective user is set, then Zope 2 will run as whoever executes the process.

You could set the `effective-user` manually or you could use the **gocept.recipe. env** recipe (`http://pypi.python.org/pypi/gocept.recipe.env`) to set it. In the case of manual configuration, you may find it tedious to test your production configuration on systems that do not have the desired effective user (or you may not; this is mostly subjective). In the case of no configuration, you may find it annoying to be reminded that you cannot run Zope 2 as root when you get to production (or you may not; this is also subjective).

In any event, we can formalize the configuration and automate the username selection process as follows.

In `07-security-effective-user.cfg`, we have:

```
[buildout]
extends = 07-security-ports.cfg
parts += env

[env]
recipe = gocept.recipe.env

[instance1]
effective-user = ${env:USER}
[instance2]
effective-user = ${env:USER}
```

Now run Buildout.

```
$ bin/buildout -c 07-security-effective-user.cfg
```

Afterward, in `parts/instance1/etc/zope.conf` you should see:

```
...
effective-user aclark
...
```

This technique has several subtle, but important advantages over manual, or no configuration:

- The effective user is always set, so even if you try to start Zope 2 as root, it will run as the effective user
- The effective user is set to the user that runs the buildout, which means you can change the effective user easily
- The `${env:USER}` variable can be used to configure user settings for additional services such as Pound, Varnish, and so on.

Installing Cassandra to audit through the web (TTW) security

If you ask anyone familiar with Plone about the permissions settings in the Security section of the Zope Management Interface, you are likely to get the following response:

"DO NOT TOUCH!"

That is because with so many possible permutations of settings, it is almost impossible to manage them all effectively by pointing and clicking.

The next thing out of their mouth is likely to be:

"USE WORKFLOW INSTEAD!"

That is because Plone's workflow feature provides a much better way to effectively manage large amounts of permission changes.

However, people do not always use workflow. They point and click away anyway, despite the warnings. You, however, have been warned. It is much better to manage permissions with workflow as compared to pointing and clicking on **Permissions** in the ZMI.

Permissions and roles in the ZMI

If you do not believe me, consider this.

If you browse to `http://localhost:8080/Plone` and click on **Site Setup | Zope Management Interface | Security**, you will see almost two hundred permissions that look like the following (first ten):

Acquire permission settings?	
☑	ATContentTypes Topic: Add ATBooleanCriterion
☑	ATContentTypes Topic: Add ATCurrentAuthorCriterion
☑	ATContentTypes Topic: Add ATDateCriteria
☑	ATContentTypes Topic: Add ATDateRangeCriterion
☑	ATContentTypes Topic: Add ATListCriterion
☑	ATContentTypes Topic: Add ATPathCriterion
☑	ATContentTypes Topic: Add ATPortalTypeCriterion
☑	ATContentTypes Topic: Add ATReferenceCriterion
☑	ATContentTypes Topic: Add ATRelativePathCriterion
☑	ATContentTypes Topic: Add ATSelectionCriterion

Next to each group of 10 permissions are checkboxes that correspond to the possible role assignments:

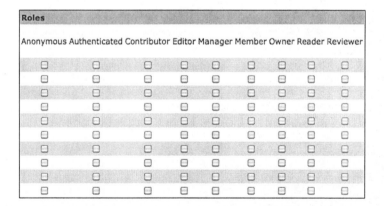

Hopefully, enough has been said. The point again is two-fold:

- The ZMI opens the gateway to enormous complexity (categorically, not just with roles and permissions)
- In the case of roles and permissions, managing this complexity is best left to workflow (in which case, role-to-permission mappings are configured by the state)

Roles and groups

Similarly, the same Plone folks will often remind you to assign roles to groups and not users, and put users in groups to enable them to perform various tasks.

They might say:

> *"DO NOT ASSIGN ROLES TO INDIVIDUAL USERS!"*

This may be followed by:

> *"ASSIGN THEM TO GROUPS INSTEAD!"*

Why? This is because to manage intricacies such as which user can perform which tasks and where, you are better off using the right tool for the job, that is adding users to groups with proper role assignments.

Unfortunately, end users are still able to assign roles to individual users if they really want to via the **Sharing** tab or **Local roles form** in the ZMI. So, it is the site manager's responsibility to make sure they do not, to avoid having a site littered with individual role assignments.

Cassandra

For the task of auditing role assignments, we have Andreas Jung's Cassandra (http://pypi.python.org/pypi/zopyx.plone.cassandra).

You can perform a local roles security audit by installing Cassandra and following the steps given below.

In 07-security-cassandra.cfg, we have:

```
[buildout]
extends = 07-security-effective-user.cfg

[instance]
eggs +=
    zopyx.plone.cassandra
zcml =
    zopyx.plone.cassandra
```

Now run Buildout:

```
$ bin/buildout -c 07-security-cassandra.cfg
```

You should see:

```
$ bin/buildout -c 07-security-cassandra.cfg
Getting distribution for 'zopyx.plone.cassandra'.
...
Got zopyx.plone.cassandra 0.2.0.
...
```

Browse to `http://localhost:8080/Plone`, click on **Site Setup | Add-on Products** to install Cassandra, and then browse to `http://localhost:8080/Plone/@@cassandra`.

On a new site, you should get no results (because no roles have been shared):

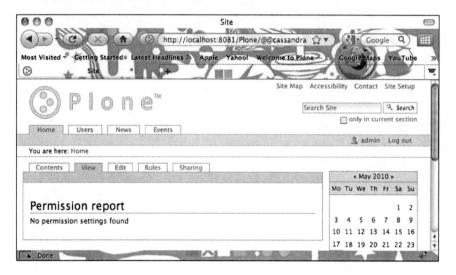

On an actively used site, you will see results similar to the following, where we use data from `http://plone.org` as an example.

For demonstration purposes, we present the output of `http://plone.org/documentation/manual/plone-3-user-manual/@@cassandra`.

In other words, we installed Cassandra on (a local copy of) plone.org, browsed to `http://localhost:8080/plone.org`, clicked on **Documentation | Manuals | Plone 3 User Manual**, and then added **@@cassandra** to the end of the URL (in the URL toolbar of your browser).

In the permission report (that took several minutes to generate), we see the following:

Current folder (Plone 3 User Manual)	▪ geojeff: ▪ DocumentationTeam: ▪ DocumentationTeamEditors: ▪ erikrose: ▪ estherschindler: ▪ gerry_kirk: ▪ inzan: ▪ natea: ▪ ree: ▪ rstephe: ▪ shurik: ▪ sknox: ▪ snowwrite: ▪ sparcd: ▪ vedawms:

Since the output is recursive, we see local role assignments for the **Current folder** and everything below it.

Here are the results for the **adding content** subfolder (that is, `/documentation/manual/plone-3-user-manual/adding-content`):

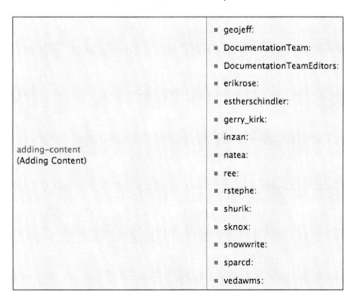

adding-content (Adding Content)	▪ geojeff: ▪ DocumentationTeam: ▪ DocumentationTeamEditors: ▪ erikrose: ▪ estherschindler: ▪ gerry_kirk: ▪ inzan: ▪ natea: ▪ ree: ▪ rstephe: ▪ shurik: ▪ sknox: ▪ snowwrite: ▪ sparcd: ▪ vedawms:

The results for the rest of the subfolders are exactly the same (except for the folder name, of course).

So what does this tell you? Several things:

- The Plone documentation team is awesome! Many people have dedicated their time and energy to writing (and rewriting) Plone's documentation for the benefit of the Plone community at large. If you know any of these folks (by their plone.org username), take a minute to thank them!
- Though the Plone documentation team members are our documentation heroes, they have (apparently) not done a good job of assigning roles to groups. Instead, they have assigned them directly to the users.
- The Cassandra output is (apparently) incomplete, as there are no roles listed after each colon. This may be due to the fact that Plone Help Center (http:// pypi.python.org/pypi/Products.PloneHelpCenter) adds additional permissions, not available in default Plone.
- All of the folders in the user manual have the same sharing settings, that is the same users and groups are listed for each folder. This suggests that local role settings are configured in a parent of the user manual folder, for example/documentation/manual or /documentation.

Applying security and bug fixes to Plone

Although it is extremely rare, vulnerabilities are found in Plone occasionally and fixes are released.

Less rare, but almost as important, are the occasional bug fix releases for various packages within the Plone software stack.

Here, we are referring to packages that contain bug fixes that were not released with a particular point release of Plone. They may also be a part of the next point release (for example, 3.3.6).

Often, you need those fixes now. Under such circumstances, it is the responsibility of all Plone site administrators to deploy these fixes to their production sites as soon as possible.

In some cases (for example with Python egg packages), the fix can be as simple as changing a package version and running Buildout to get the latest compatible release (which presumably addresses the security, or the bug issue).

In other cases, alternative methods are required.

Such was the case with the last known Zope 2 security issue, which occurred in early 2010 (`http://cve.mitre.org/cgi-bin/cvename.cgi?name=CVE-2010-1104`).

Since many of the affected Plone sites had old style (non-egg package) Zope 2 software installations, that is, Zope 2 was installed from the gzipped and tarred source archive instead of using a "versionable" egg (starting from Zope 2.12, Zope 2 is packaged as an egg), it was necessary to update the URL of the Zope 2 source distribution in the buildout.

Using a newer Zope 2 with an older release of Plone

To demonstrate this, we are going to run an older (unsupported) version of Plone (2.1) with a newer version of Zope 2 (much newer than the version of Zope 2 Plone 2.1 was originally released with).

In general, it is safe to use the newest point release in a series. At the time of writing this, the newest point release for each (actively-maintained) series of Zope 2 releases is as follows:

- `http://www.zope.org/Products/Zope/2.8.12/Zope-2.8.12-final.tgz`
- `http://www.zope.org/Products/Zope/2.9.12/Zope-2.9.12-final.tgz`
- `http://www.zope.org/Products/Zope/2.10.11/Zope-2.10.11-final.tgz`
- `http://www.zope.org/Products/Zope/2.11.5/Zope-2.11.5-final.tgz`
- `http://pypi.python.org/packages/source/Z/Zope2/Zope2-2.12.6.zip`

Hold on to your buildouts

Throughout this book, we have built incrementally on examples from the previous chapter and from previous examples in the same chapter. As such, we were extending a single buildout all the time.

Because it does not extend any of the previous configuration files, when you run this example, it will undo everything that has been done before.

As such, you may wish to copy the `07-security-plone21.cfg` file to another directory and run it from there instead. You have been warned!

Generally speaking, it is always a good idea to keep in mind that Buildout maintains its state. So whenever you execute Buildout, you are asking it to modify its state. Hopefully, you are giving it sensible instructions, but humans are often flawed; we make silly mistakes. The good news is that if you make a mistake, it is almost always easily undone simply by executing Buildout again with the correct configuration file.

A "modern" Plone 2.1 buildout

In `07-security-plone21.cfg`, we have:

```
[buildout]
find-links = http://dist.plone.org/thirdparty/PILwoTk-1.1.6.4.tar.gz
versions = versions
parts =
    instance
    plone

[zope2]
recipe = plone.recipe.zope2install
url = http://www.zope.org/Products/Zope/2.8.12/Zope-2.8.12-final.tgz

[plone]
recipe = hexagonit.recipe.download
url = http://dist.plone.org/archive/Plone-2.1.4.tar.gz
strip-top-level-dir = true

[instance]
recipe = plone.recipe.zope2instance
zope2-location = ${zope2:location}
user = admin:admin
eggs =
    PILwoTk
products =
    ${buildout:directory}/parts/plone

[versions]
plone.recipe.zope2instance = 3.6
```

You will notice that we specify the version of Zope 2 to install by setting the value of the url parameter to the URL of the Zope 2 gzipped and tarred archive on zope.org.

We use Zope 2.8.12 because it is the newest version of Zope 2 that will work with the very old release of Plone, Plone 2.1.4.

We demonstrate this for one very important reason—to empower you to upgrade your Zope 2 installations in the event that a security issue is discovered. If and when this happens, a subsequent new version of Zope 2 will be released to address the issue, and you will need to know how to install it.

In case of many other packages (that is, those which are packaged as eggs) as we mentioned earlier, getting a newer package is often just a matter of specifying which version you want to install in your buildout.

Incidentally, we have not discussed in detail how to specify package versions yet (beyond specifying version numbers for Plone and its dependencies via the `versions.cfg` file), but we will get to that in the next (and final) chapter.

Summary

That is all for this important chapter. Here you have learned:

- How to restrict TCP/IP access to localhost only
- How to manage IP addresses and ports effectively with Buildout sections
- How to configure the Zope 2 effective user dynamically with gocept.recipe.env
- How to audit Plone security settings with Cassandra
- How to upgrade Zope 2 in the event of a security or bug fix release

Up next we will enter the final chapter, wherein we will demonstrate an upgrade to Plone 4, summarize everything we have learned so far, and wrap up with a few important points we have not had the opportunity to discuss yet.

See you there!

8
The Future

We have spent a great deal of time demonstrating how to use Buildout to develop, deploy, and maintain Plone sites with a wide variety of.

Now we would like to leave you with a clear path to Plone 4, which is likely to be released around the time this book is published.

It is likely that some of the add-ons we have used in this book do not yet have a corresponding Plone 4 compatible release. We will address that as well.

Before we can safely blast off, we must ensure that our buildouts will execute as successfully in the future as they do now.

In this chapter you will learn:

- Specifying package versions
- Executing Buildout in offline mode
- Analyzing our buildout's contents
- Staying calm when trouble arises
- Upgrading to Plone 4

Specifying package versions

We have discussed numerous Buildout recipes in this book, but no Buildout extensions (`http://pypi.python.org/pypi/zc.buildout#extensions`) until now. A Buildout extension is different from a recipe in a few important ways:

- Extensions do not define any new sections, whereas recipes are often used within a section (although a section can be defined without a recipe)
- Extensions are run after Buildout reads its configuration files, but before it executes them
- Extensions are defined within the buildout section

That being said, you do not need to worry too much about the difference; just be aware of which one you are using.

If you know something is an extension, then it should be defined in the `buildout` section. If it is a recipe, it should be defined in its own section.

We are going to use the **buildout.dumppickedversions** (`http://pypi.python.org/pypi/buildout.dumppickedversions`) extension to help us figure out which package's versions are unspecified (which means effectively, we are asking for the latest version).

Logically, we know that versions are unspecified for any package we have added since we configured Plone 3.3.5's package versions in `buildout.cfg`:

```
[buildout]
extends = http://dist.plone.org/release/3.3.5/versions.cfg
versions = versions
...
```

You may also recall that we assigned the `versions` section from `http://dist.plone.org/release/3.3.5/versions.cfg` to our buildout's `versions` section with `versions = versions`.

Now we are going to add the buildout.dumppickedversions extension to our `buildout`, run Buildout, and examine the output.

In `08-future-dumppicked.cfg`, we have:

```
[buildout]
extends = 07-security-cassandra.cfg
extensions = buildout.dumppickedversions
```

Now run Buildout:

```
$ bin/buildout -c 08-future-dumppicked.cfg
```

You should see:

```
$ bin/buildout -c 08-future-dumppicked.cfg
Getting distribution for buildout.dumppickedversions.
Got buildout.dumppickedversions 0.4.
************** PICKED VERSIONS ****************
[versions]
Cheetah = 2.2.1
Paste = 1.7.3.1
```

```
Products.CacheSetup = 1.2.1

...


#Required by:
#PasteScript 1.7.3
PasteDeploy = 1.3.3


#Required by:
#ZopeSkel 2.16
PasteScript = 1.7.3


#Required by:
#Products.CacheSetup 1.2.1
Products.CMFSquidTool = 1.5.1

...
```

```
*************** /PICKED VERSIONS ***************
```

This is incredibly useful information.

Assuming that Buildout is executed successfully, and your Plone site works as expected, we can now add all of this version information to our `buildout`, and be reasonably confident that it will continue to execute successfully.

Without a complete and working **Known Good Set** (**KGS**), there exists the possibility that a newer package will be released to the Python Package Index that is not compatible with the rest of our KGS.

This would effectively mean one of the two things, the former of which is more likely:

- Buildout would fail to complete, citing a version conflict
- Buildout would complete, but your Plone site would not start citing a traceback

To avoid this, we use a KGS of packages whenever possible.

Because we specified `versions = versions` in `buildout.cfg`, we can add additional `versions` blocks as needed.

In `08-future-versions.cfg`, we have:

```
[buildout]
extends = 08-future-dumppicked.cfg

[versions]
Cheetah = 2.2.1
Paste = 1.7.3.1
Products.CacheSetup = 1.2.1
...

#Required by:
#PasteScript 1.7.3
PasteDeploy = 1.3.3

#Required by:
#ZopeSkel 2.16
PasteScript = 1.7.3

#Required by:
#Products.CacheSetup 1.2.1
Products.CMFSquidTool = 1.5.1


...
```

Now, run Buildout:

$ bin/buildout -c 08-future-dumppicked.cfg

You should see:

$ bin/buildout -c 08-future-dumppicked.cfg

...

**************** PICKED VERSIONS ****************

[versions]

ZopeSkel = 2.16

************** /PICKED VERSIONS ***************

You will notice that buildout.dumppickedversions no longer picks any versions (except for ZopeSkel, which may be a bug, as version 2.16 is specified).

Executing Buildout in offline mode

Specifying package versions is critical to creating a KGS.

So, what happens if the Internet goes down and/or you are unable to reach `http://dist.plone.org/release/3.3.5/versions.cfg`?

For this, we have two approaches.

The first, newer approach is to use Buildout's **extends cache** feature, information about which is available on `http://pypi.python.org/pypi/zc.buildout#caching-extended-configuration`. We will not cover that here, but it is probably worth a look.

In the worst-case scenario though, you can try the following approach.

Inside the code bundle in the `versions.cfg` file, we have included the contents of `http://dist.plone.org/release/3.3.5/versions.cfg`.

In the event you lose connectivity, or you want to deploy to an environment sans Internet, you need two things:

- The packages themselves (which reside in the `eggs` directory)
- Their version specifications

We already included version specifications for our add-on packages in `08-future-versions.cfg`, which we discovered with buildout.dumppickedversions.

Now, we will specify the Plone 3.3.5 package versions in our local `versions.cfg`, rather than the `versions.cfg` file located on `http://dist.plone.org/release/3.3.5/versions.cfg`. In `buildout.cfg`, we have:

```
[buildout]
extends = http://dist.plone.org/release/3.3.5/versions.cfg
versions = versions
...
```

If you add a comment (#) to the beginning of the second line and then add `extends = versions.cfg` below that, you will have this:

```
[buildout]
#extends = http://dist.plone.org/release/3.3.5/versions.cfg
extends = versions.cfg
versions = versions
...
```

Now execute the last known good configuration with the -o option to indicate offline mode.

You should see:

```
$ bin/buildout -o -c 08-future-versions.cfg
Updating zope2.
Updating fake eggs
Updating instance.
Updating omelette.
...
Updating zopepy.
Updating zopeskel.
Updating zeo.
Updating backup.
Updating cron.
Updating cron2.
Updating varnish-install.
Updating varnish.
Updating squid-install.
Updating squid.
Updating env.
Updating instance1.
Updating instance2.
Updating haproxy-install.
Updating haproxy-config.
Updating pound-install.
Updating pound-config.
Updating supervisor.
Updating munin.
...
```

In other words, it should execute successfully.

Analyzing the contents of our buildout

In this book, we have created a fairly large buildout, spread across many files. As a result, perhaps you are wondering what it would look like if the same buildout were contained in a single file?

We answer that question in `08-future-final.cfg`, which contains the following sections, parameters, and values, presented here along with some commentary about each:

- Every buildout must define a `buildout` section:

  `[buildout]`

- By assigning parameters from various `versions` sections to the `versions` parameter in the `buildout` section, we are able to specify package version numbers:

  `versions = versions`

- Every `buildout` section must have a `parts` parameter (even if it is empty):

  ```
  parts =
      zope2
      instance
  ```

- In *Chapter 2, Site Basics*, we introduced the collective.recipe.plonesite recipe (`http://pypi.python.org/pypi/collective.recipe.plonesite`) configured in a section called `plonesite`:

  ```
  # Chapter 2
      plonesite
  ```

- In *Chapter 3, Appearance*, we introduced the collective.recipe.omelette recipe (`http://pypi.python.org/pypi/collective.recipe.omelette`) configured in a section called `omelette`. We also demonstrated the use of the zc.recipe.egg recipe (`http://pypi.python.org/pypi/zc.recipe.egg`) in the `zopepy` and `zopeskel` sections:

  ```
  # Chapter 3
      omelette
      zopepy
      zopeskel
  ```

- In *Chapter 5, Deployment and Maintenance*, we introduced the collective.recipe. backup recipe (`http://pypi.python.org/pypi/collective.recipe. backup`) to generate scripts to back up your Plone site's database and also introduced the z3c.recipe.usercrontab recipe (`http://pypi.python.org/ pypi/z3c.recipe.usercrontab`) to automate the execution of these scripts.

- We also discussed using the plone.recipe.zope2zeoserver recipe (`http://pypi.python.org/pypi/plone.recipe.zope2zeoserver`) to configure a ZEO server:

```
# Chapter 5
    backup
    cron
    cron2
    zeo
```

- In *Chapter 6, Optimization*, for the purpose of site optimization, we demonstrated the use of the collective.recipe.supervisor (`http://pypi.python.org/pypi/collective.recipe.supervisor`), collective.recipe.template (`http://pypi.python.org/pypi/collective.recipe.template`), hexagonit.recipe.cmmi (`http://pypi.python.org/pypi/hexagonit.recipe.cmmi`), plone.recipe.haproxy (`http://pypi.python.org/pypi/plone.recipe.haproxy`), plone.recipe.squid (`http://pypi.python.org/pypi/plone.recipe.squid`), plone.recipe.varnish (`http://pypi.python.org/pypi/plone.recipe.varnish`), zc.recipe.cmmi (`http://pypi.python.org/pypi/zc.recipe.cmmi`), and zc.recipe.egg recipes within the following sections.

```
# Chapter 6
    instance1
    instance2
    haproxy-install
    haproxy-config
    pound-install
    pound-config
    munin
    squid-install
    squid
    varnish-install
    varnish
    supervisor
```

- We also demonstrated the use of Buildout macros.

- In *Chapter 7, Security*, we demonstrated the use of the gocept.recipe.env recipe (`http://pypi.python.org/pypi/gocept.recipe.env`) to configure the Zope 2 effective user dynamically:

```
# Chapter 7
    env
```

- In Chapter 3, we demonstrated how to add a ZopeSkel-generated (`http://pypi.python.org/pypi/ZopeSkel`) theme package to your buildout:

```
# Chapter 3
develop = src/my.theme
```

- In this chapter, we demonstrated how to get a list of packages whose versions have not been specified, by using the buildout.dumppickedversions Buildout extension (`http://pypi.python.org/pypi/buildout.dumppickedversions`):

```
# Chapter 8
extensions = buildout.dumppickedversions
```

- In Chapter 2, we introduced the Plone buildout (in `buildout.cfg`), which uses the plone.recipe.zope2install (`http://pypi.python.org/pypi/plone.recipe.zope2install`) and plone.recipe.zope2instance (`http://pypi.python.org/pypi/plone.recipe.zope2instance`) recipes to install Zope 2 and configure a Zope 2 instance, respectively:

```
[zope2]
recipe = plone.recipe.zope2install
url = ${versions:zope2-url}


[instance]
recipe = plone.recipe.zope2instance
zope2-location = ${zope2:location}
user = admin:admin
eggs =
    Plone
```

- In Chapter 2, for the purpose of site theming, we added the following packages to the `eggs` parameter of the `instance` section:

```
# Chapter 2
    Products.Scrawl
    webcouturier.dropdownmenu
    collective.portlet.explore
    collective.portlet.sitemap
```

- In Chapter 3, we created and demonstrated the use of a very simple theme package on the filesystem:

```
# Chapter 3
    my.theme
```

- In Chapter 3, we installed an attractive add-on theme package:

```
# Chapter 3
    beyondskins.ploneday.site2010
```

- In *Chapter 4, Administration*, we demonstrated user and group management with LDAP, as well as how to configure Zope 2 to send a mail to the terminal:

```
# Chapter 4
    plone.app.ldap
#     Products.PrintingMailHost
```

- In Chapter 5, we demonstrated how to rotate Zope 2 log files with iw.rotatezlogs (`http://pypi.python.org/pypi/iw.rotatezlogs`):

```
# Chapter 5
    iw.rotatezlogs
```

- In Chapter 6, we demonstrated how to configure various cache-related settings easily with the CacheFu (`http://pypi.python.org/pypi/Products.CacheSetup`) add-on. We also demonstrated how to produce useful site monitoring graphs with munin.zope (`http://pypi.python.org/pypi/munin.zope`) and Munin:

```
# Chapter 6
    Products.CacheSetup
    munin.zope
```

- In Chapter 7, we demonstrated how to perform a local roles audit with Cassandra (`http://pypi.python.org/pypi/zopyx.plone.cassandra`):

```
# Chapter 7
    zopyx.plone.cassandra
```

- In the various chapters, we explained the need to configure the `zcml` parameter in the `instance` section:

```
zcml =
# Chapter 2
    webcouturier.dropdownmenu
    collective.portlet.explore
    collective.portlet.sitemap
# Chapter 3
    beyondskins.ploneday.site2010
# Chapter 4
    plone.app.ldap
# Chapter 6
    munin.zope
# Chapter 7
    zopyx.plone.cassandra
```

- Once we added the iw.rotatezlogs package to the `eggs` parameter of the `instance` section, we added these parameters to the `instance` section (which configure additional settings in the `zope.conf` file):

```
# Chapter 5
zeo-client = True
event-log-custom =
    %import iw.rotatezlogs
    <rotatelogfile>
        path ${buildout:directory}/var/log/instance.log
        max-bytes 1MB
        backup-count 5
    </rotatelogfile>
access-log-custom =
    %import iw.rotatezlogs
    <rotatelogfile>
        path ${buildout:directory}/var/log/instance-Z2.log
        max-bytes 1MB
        backup-count 5
    </rotatelogfile>
```

- The `plonesite` section adds and configures a Plone site in the database whenever Buildout runs:

```
# Chapter 2
[plonesite]
recipe = collective.recipe.plonesite
site-id = Plone
```

- The `omelette` section creates symbolic links from the `parts/omelette` directory to various packages elsewhere on the filesystem:

```
# Chapter 3
[omelette]
recipe = collective.recipe.omelette
eggs = ${instance:eggs}
packages = ${zope2:location}/lib/python
```

- The `zopepy` section creates a `bin/zopepy` script (Python interpreter) with the instance packages and Zope 2 libraries added to `sys.path`:

```
[zopepy]
recipe = zc.recipe.egg
eggs = ${instance:eggs}
interpreter = zopepy
extra-paths = ${zope2:location}/lib/python
scripts = zopepy
```

- The `zopeskel` section installs ZopeSkel in the buildout:

```
[zopeskel]
recipe = zc.recipe.egg
dependent-scripts = true
```

- The `backup`, `cron`, and `cron2` sections create backup scripts and `cron` entries for the purpose of performing backups:

```
# Chapter 5
[backup]
recipe = collective.recipe.backup


[cron]
recipe = z3c.recipe.usercrontab
command = ${buildout:directory}/bin/backup
times = 0 0 * * *


[cron2]
recipe = z3c.recipe.usercrontab
command = ${buildout:directory}/bin/zeopack
times = 0 0 1 * *
```

- The `zeo` section installs a ZEO instance:

```
[zeo]
recipe = plone.recipe.zope2zeoserver
zope2-location = ${zope2:location}
eggs = ${instance:eggs}
zeo-log-custom =
    %import iw.rotatezlogs
    <rotatelogfile>
        path ${buildout:directory}/var/log/zeo.log
        max-bytes 1MB
        backup-count 5
    </rotatelogfile>
```

- The `haproxy-config` section uses the collective.recipe.template recipe to generate a template for HAProxy dynamically, based on the contents of an input template:

```
# Chapter 6
[haproxy-config]
recipe = collective.recipe.template
input = ${buildout:directory}/templates/haproxy.cfg.in
output = ${buildout:directory}/etc/haproxy.cfg
```

- The `haproxy-install` section downloads and installs HAProxy (which unfortunately cannot be compiled with any of the available CMMI recipes (such as zc.recipe.cmmi) as you may expect it to be):

```
[haproxy-install]
recipe = plone.recipe.haproxy
```

- The `instance1` and `instance2` sections demonstrate the use of Buildout macros to easily create duplicate instances based on the `instance` section, with various parameters changed or added as needed:

```
[instance1]
< = instance
http-address = 8081
# Chapter 7
effective-user = ${env:USER}
http-address = 127.0.0.1:8081

[instance2]
< = instance
http-address = 8082
# Chapter 7
effective-user = ${env:USER}
http-address = 127.0.0.1:8082
```

- The `munin` section configures a `bin/munin` script that is used to generate symbolic links from your site's Munin plugins directory to `bin/munin` (which in turn, produces appropriate output for Munin, based on how it is invoked, that is with the various symbol links).

```
[munin]
recipe = zc.recipe.egg
eggs = munin.zope
arguments =
    http_address=${instance1:http-address},
    user=${instance1:user}
```

- The `pound-config` section uses the collective.recipe.template recipe to generate a template for Pound dynamically based on the contents of an input template:

```
[pound-config]
recipe = collective.recipe.template
input = ${buildout:directory}/templates/pound.cfg.in
output = ${buildout:directory}/etc/pound.cfg
```

- The `pound-install` section uses the hexagonit.recipe.cmmi recipe to download and install Pound:

```
[pound-install]
recipe = hexagonit.recipe.cmmi
url = http://www.apsis.ch/pound/Pound-2.4.5.tgz
make-targets =
keep-compile-dir = true
```

- The `squid-install` section uses the zc.recipe.cmmi recipe to download and install Squid:

```
[squid-install]
recipe = zc.recipe.cmmi
url = http://www.squid-cache.org/Versions/v2/2.7/squid-
2.7.STABLE9.tar.gz
```

- The `squid` section uses the plone.recipe.squid recipe to configure a Squid configuration file:

```
[squid]
recipe = plone.recipe.squid:instance
cache-size = 1000
daemon = ${squid-install:location}/sbin/squid
backends = 127.0.0.1:8080
bind = 127.0.0.1:3128
```

- The following sections provide friendly variable names to access some unfriendly in-length parameters:

```
[pound]
directory = ${buildout:directory}/parts/pound-install__compile__
config = ${pound:directory}/etc/pound.cfg
[haproxy]
config = ${buildout:directory}/etc/haproxy.cfg
```

- The `supervisor` section configures Supervisor to execute and control all the services in our buildout:

```
[supervisor]
recipe = collective.recipe.supervisor
programs =
#Prio    Name        Program                                    Params
  00     zeo         ${zeo:location}/bin/runzeo
  00     instance1   ${instance1:location}/bin/runzope
  00     instance2   ${instance2:location}/bin/runzope
  00     haproxy     ${buildout:directory}/bin/haproxy\
    [-f ${haproxy:config} ]
```

```
00        pound        ${pound:directory}/Pound-2.4.5/pound\
  [-f ${pound:config} ]
00        varnish      ${buildout:directory}/bin/varnish      [-F]
00        squid        ${buildout:directory}/bin/squid        [-N]
```

- The `varnish-install` section uses the zc.recipe.cmmi recipe to download and install Varnish:

```
[varnish-install]
recipe = zc.recipe.cmmi
url = http://downloads.sourceforge.net/project/varnish/varnish/\
      2.1.2/varnish-2.1.2.tar.gz
```

- The `varnish` section uses the plone.recipe.varnish recipe to create a Varnish configuration file:

```
[varnish]
recipe = plone.recipe.varnish
daemon = ${varnish-install:location}/sbin/varnishd
```

- The `env` section provides access to the operating system shell's environment variables (for example, USER):

```
[env]
recipe = gocept.recipe.env
```

- The `hosts` and `ports` sections provide a way to standardize and easily control IP address and port settings:

```
# Chapter 7
[hosts]
localhost = 127.0.0.1

[ports]
instance1 = 8081
instance2 = 8082
```

- In this chapter, we discussed how to configure package versions in part, by specifying version numbers in a `versions` section (and also by setting `versions` = `versions` in the `buildout` section):

```
# Chapter 8
[versions]
Cheetah = 2.2.1
Paste = 1.7.3.1
Products.CacheSetup = 1.2.1
...

#Required by:
```

```
#PasteScript 1.7.3
PasteDeploy = 1.3.3

#Required by:
#ZopeSkel 2.16
PasteScript = 1.7.3

#Required by:
#Products.CacheSetup 1.2.1
Products.CMFSquidTool = 1.5.1

...

# Buildout infrastructure
plone.recipe.zope2install = 3.2
plone.recipe.zope2instance = 3.6
plone.recipe.zope2zeoserver = 1.4
setuptools = 0.6c11
zc.buildout = 1.4.3
zc.recipe.egg = 1.2.2

# Zope
zope2-url =
  http://www.zope.org/Products/Zope/2.10.11/Zope-2.10.11-final.tgz

# External dependencies
Markdown = 1.7
PIL = 1.1.6
elementtree = 1.2.7-20070827-preview
feedparser = 4.1
python-openid = 2.2.4
simplejson = 2.0.9

# Plone release
Plone = 3.3.5
Products.ATContentTypes = 1.3.4
Products.ATReferenceBrowserWidget = 2.0.5
...
```

For whatever it is worth, this is the final buildout example (before we blast off in to the future) that demonstrates all the functionality we have added incrementally with each chapter.

Ideally, you can browse through 08-future-final.cfg and when you see something you do not understand, refer to the corresponding chapter for an explanation.

Staying calm when trouble arises

It is a harsh reality that while experimenting with your Plone buildout (such as adding various packages from the Python Package Index), things are more likely to go wrong than they are to go right.

Do yourself a favor and:

1. Do not panic.
2. Paste the error message to `http://paste.plone.org`.
3. Join the #plone IRC channel on `irc://irc.freenode.net/` and ask the folks in there if they understand the error.
4. Alternatively, ask a question on the Plone users' mailing list on Sourceforge. net (`https://lists.sourceforge.net/lists/listinfo/plone-users`).

A lot of times, what appears to be a cryptic error is actually not to the trained eye. It is important that you learn to tell the difference.

You can read more about the available support options for Plone on `http://plone.org/support`.

The Plone community is a thoughtful and generous one, so you will be welcomed and encouraged to learn!

Upgrading to Plone 4

It is now time to explore upgrading to Plone 4.

Nowadays, as far as the software itself is concerned, this is a relatively simple process.

Especially as far as our `buildout.cfg` file is concerned, it is simple.

At the time of this writing, Plone 4 is just about to release its first release candidate. This means that we can experiment with the most recent beta release — beta 3.

For Plone 4 beta 3's versions.cfg file, visit `http://dist.plone.org/release/4.0b3/versions.cfg`.

Even though we have already specified a `versions.cfg`, we can specify another one, because Buildout will just use the last specified value for each parameter.

In the case of a `versions` section that looks like as shown, Buildout will use the latter version:

```
[versions]
Plone = 3.3.5
Plone = 4.0b3
```

Effectively, extending the Plone 4 beta 3 `versions.cfg` file and executing Buildout upgrades your software stack (but not your database) to Plone 4 beta 3.

There are a few additional concerns we must address before you do that.

1. First, and most importantly, you must re-bootstrap your buildout with Python 2.6, as shown:

    ```
    $ python2.6 bootstrap.py
    ```

2. Second, you must backup your database (which you learned how to do in Chapter 5).

3. Third, you must uninstall the add-ons for which there is no Plone 4 compatible release. In our case, we must uninstall all the add-ons (more or less).

4. Fourth, you will browse to `http://localhost:8080/Plone`, click on **Site Setup | Add-on Products** and uninstall all the add-ons we had installed.

    Ideally, this process will be trouble-free, though often it is not. In the event you have trouble uninstalling an add-on, you should contact the author.

5. Fifth, we are going to subtract all the sections and parameters that are not absolutely essential to run Plone 4, from our buildout. That means everything but the `instance` section is to be subtracted.

6. Finally, you will execute the buildout.

In `08-future-plone4.cfg` we have:

```
[buildout]
extends =
    08-future-final.cfg
    http://dist.plone.org/release/4.0b3/versions.cfg

develop =

parts -=
    zope2
    omelette
    zopepy
    zopeskel
```

```
    backup
    cron
    cron2
    zeo
    instance1
    instance2
    haproxy-install
    haproxy-config
    pound-install
    pound-config
    munin
    squid-install
    squid
    varnish-install
    varnish
    supervisor

[instance]
zope2-location =
eggs -=
    Products.Scrawl
    webcouturier.dropdownmenu
    collective.portlet.explore
    collective.portlet.sitemap
    my.theme
    beyondskins.ploneday.site2010
    plone.app.ldap
    iw.rotatezlogs
    Products.CacheSetup
    munin.zope
    zopyx.plone.cassandra

event-log-custom =
access-log-custom =
zeo-client =
```

Now run Buildout:

```
$ bin/buildout -c 08-future-plone4.cfg
```

This Buildout should complete successfully. However, in the real world you do not have to go to the trouble of subtracting out all the Plone 3 parts of your buildout. You can just use a real Plone 4 buildout.

In `08-future-just-plone4.cfg`, we have:

```
[buildout]
extends = http://dist.plone.org/release/4.0b3/versions.cfg
versions = versions
parts = instance

[instance]
recipe = plone.recipe.zope2instance
user = admin:admin
eggs = Plone
```

Now run Buildout:

$ bin/buildout -c 08-future-just-plone4.cfg

You should see:

Installing instance.

Generated script /Users/aclark/Developer/plone-site-admin/buildout/bin/instance.

Start Plone:

$ bin/instance fg

You should see:

```
$ bin/instance fg
2010-05-24 22:42:24 INFO ZServer HTTP server started at Mon May 24
22:42:24 2010
  Hostname: localhost
  Port: 8080
2010-05-24 22:42:27 INFO ZODB.blob (31597) Blob directory `/Users/aclark/
Developer/plone-site-admin/buildout/var/blobstorage` is unused and has no
layout marker set. Selected `bushy` layout.
2010-05-24 22:42:27 INFO ZODB.blob (31597) Blob temporary directory /
Users/aclark/Developer/plone-site-admin/buildout/var/blobstorage/tmp does
not exist. Created new directory.
2010-05-24 22:42:27 WARNING ZODB.blob (31597) Blob dir /Users/aclark/
Developer/plone-site-admin/buildout/var/blobstorage/ has insecure mode
setting
/Users/aclark/Developer/eggs/Zope2-2.12.5-py2.6-macosx-
10.6-x86_64.egg/Zope2/App/ClassFactory.py:22: DeprecationWarning:
PlacelessTranslationService: The PlacelessTranslationService itself is
deprecated and will be removed in the next major version of PTS.
  return getattr(m, name)
2010-05-24 22:42:31 WARNING OFS.Uninstalled Could not import class
TextIndex from module Products.PluginIndexes.TextIndex.TextIndex
```

```
/Users/aclark/Developer/eggs/Zope2-2.12.5-py2.6-macosx-10.6-x86_64.egg/
Zope2/App/ClassFactory.py:22: DeprecationWarning: BrokenMessageCatalog:
PlacelessTranslationServices implementation of Message catalogs and the
MoFileCache is deprecated and will be removed in the next major version
of PTS.
  return getattr(m, name)
2010-05-24 22:42:32 INFO Zope Ready to handle requests
```

Browse to `http://localhost:8080/` (not `http://localhost:8080/Plone`).

You should see:

Click on **Upgrade**. You should see:

Now click on **Site**.

Summary

In this final chapter, you have learned:

- How to specify package versions, with help from a Buildout extension
- How to execute Buildout successfully when no Internet connection is available
- How to create and manage a complex buildout in one or many files
- How to upgrade Plone and manage the complexities of the process
- What to do when errors occur

In this book, you have hopefully learned how to manage your Plone site using Buildout and related tools. Your potential to build attractive, multi-functional websites with Plone is limitless.

Assembling Plone applications with Buildout is a complex task, but one that can be managed effectively without too much complexity.

The author hopes you have enjoyed reading this book, and wishes you all the best with your Plone sites!

Index

Symbols

${} notation 48
__iinit__.pyo file 88
__init__.py file 87, 88
-= notation 131
.py 53
.pyc 53
+= syntax 56

A

Active Directory (AD) 117
Amazon EC2, URL 147
asterisk (*) field 137

B

backup section 202
blog entry type, Plone
  about 68-71
  blog_view, configuring 71, 72
  RSS feed, configuring 73, 74
blog_view, blog entry type
  adding, to Plone site 72
  configuring 71, 72
Bluebream 7
browser/ directory 88
bug fixes
  applying, to Plone 186
Buildout
  about 43
  contents, analyzing 197-206
  executing, in offline mode 195, 196
  file format, configuring 44
  global versus local buildout command 45

HAProxy 160, 161
installing 27
installing, on Mac OS X 27, 28
installing, on Ubuntu Linux 29
installing, on Windows 7 28
Munin plug-ins 168
plone.app.ldap, adding 118, 119
Plone site, adding 53
Plone site, adding with 56-58
Pound 163
Python buildout 44
themes, adding with 78, 79
themes, installing with 77
Varnish, installing 153-156
ZopeSkel, adding 90, 92
buildout command 45
buildout.dumppickedversions extension
    192
Buildout macros
  multiple instances, creating 158, 159
buildout section, Python buildout 44

C

CacheFu
  installing 149-153
Cassandra
  about 183, 185
  installing, audit through the web (TTW)
      security 181
C compiler
  installing 31
  installing, on Mac OS X 31
  installing, on Ubuntu Linux 34
  installing, on Windows 32

Thank you for buying
Plone 3.3 Site Administration

About Packt Publishing

Packt, pronounced 'packed', published its first book "*Mastering phpMyAdmin for Effective MySQL Management*" in April 2004 and subsequently continued to specialize in publishing highly focused books on specific technologies and solutions.

Our books and publications share the experiences of your fellow IT professionals in adapting and customizing today's systems, applications, and frameworks. Our solution based books give you the knowledge and power to customize the software and technologies you're using to get the job done. Packt books are more specific and less general than the IT books you have seen in the past. Our unique business model allows us to bring you more focused information, giving you more of what you need to know, and less of what you don't.

Packt is a modern, yet unique publishing company, which focuses on producing quality, cutting-edge books for communities of developers, administrators, and newbies alike. For more information, please visit our website: www.packtpub.com.

About Packt Open Source

In 2010, Packt launched two new brands, Packt Open Source and Packt Enterprise, in order to continue its focus on specialization. This book is part of the Packt Open Source brand, home to books published on software built around Open Source licences, and offering information to anybody from advanced developers to budding web designers. The Open Source brand also runs Packt's Open Source Royalty Scheme, by which Packt gives a royalty to each Open Source project about whose software a book is sold.

Writing for Packt

We welcome all inquiries from people who are interested in authoring. Book proposals should be sent to author@packtpub.com. If your book idea is still at an early stage and you would like to discuss it first before writing a formal book proposal, contact us; one of our commissioning editors will get in touch with you.

We're not just looking for published authors; if you have strong technical skills but no writing experience, our experienced editors can help you develop a writing career, or simply get some additional reward for your expertise.

open source*
community experience distilled

Practical Plone 3

A Beginner's Guide to Building Powerful Websites

Practical Plone 3: A Beginner's Guide to Building Powerful Websites

ISBN: 978-1-847191-78-6   Paperback: 592 pages

A beginner's practical guide to building Plone websites through graphical interface

1. Get a Plone-based website up and running quickly without dealing with code

2. Beginner's guide with easy-to-follow instructions and screenshots

3. Learn how to make the best use of Plone's out-of-the-box features

Plone 3 Theming

Create flexible, powerful, and professional themes for your web site with Plone and basic CSS

Veda Williams

Plone 3 Theming

ISBN: 978-1-847193-87-2   Paperback: 324 pages

Create flexible, powerful, and professional themes for your web site with Plone and basic CSS

1. Best practices for creating a flexible and powerful Plone themes

2. Build new templates and refactor existing ones by using Plone's templating system, Zope Page Templates (ZPT) system, Template Attribute Language (TAL) tricks and tips for skinning your Plone site

3. Create a fully functional theme to ensure proper understanding of all the concepts

Please check **www.PacktPub.com** for information on our titles

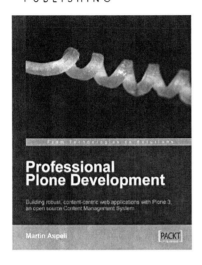

Breinigsville, PA USA
29 July 2010
242620BV00004B/17/P